A Family Hour Fun Book

John C. Souter & James O'Brosky

Harvest House Publishers
Eugene, Oregon 97402

OTHER BOOKS BY THE AUTHOR:

Personal Bible Study Notebook Vol. 1 (Tyndale House Publishers)
Personal Bible Study Notebook Vol. 11 (Tyndale House Publishers)
Personal Prayer Notebook (Tyndale House Publishers)
Youth Bible Study Notebook (Tyndale House Publishers)
Christian In Today's Society (Tyndale House Publishers)
Jesus From Nazareth: Liberator? (Inspiration House)
Jesus From Nazareth: Liberator? Bible study guide (Inspiration House)
The Pleasure Seller (Tyndale and Inspiration House Publishers)
Grow! (Tyndale House Pubishers)
How To Grow New Christians (Tyndale House Publishers)
Tales of Jeremy Hopper (Tyndale House Publishers)

Scripture quotations marked TLB are from THE LIVING BIBLE, copyright © 1971, Tyndale House Publishers, Wheaton, Illinois. Used by permission.

Scripture quotations marked NASB are from the NEW AMERICAN STANDARD BIBLE, © The Lockman Foundation 1960, 1962, 1963, 1968, 1971, 1972, 1973, 1975 and are used by permission.

A FAMILY HOUR FUNBOOK (formerly called A FAMILY HOUR NOTEBOOK).

Copyright © 1978 John C. Souter
Published by Harvest House Publishers
Eugene, Oregon 97402
Library of Congress Catalog Card Number: 78-56877
ISBN 0-89081-357-4

All rights reserved. No portion of this book may be reproduced in any form without the written permission of the publisher.

Printed in the United States of America.

— Contents —

Introduction   5
    Why Have A Family Hour?
    What The Family Hour is Not
    Family Hour Organization
    How to Begin
    Notes to The Pastor

Teaching Material
  I. **Getting to Know God**   8
     1. Can You Know God?   8
     2. Meeting God   10
  II. **Getting to Know God Better**   14
     3. Bible Study: Listening to God   14
     4. Prayer: Talking to God   18
     5. Fellowship: Enjoying God Together   20
  III. **People Who Knew God**   23
     6. Abraham Trusted God   23
     7. Daniel Prayed   25
     8. Paul Gave His All   28
  IV. **Who Is God?**   30
     9. God the Father   30
    10. God the Son   33
    11. God the Holy Spirit   36
    12. The Three-in-Oneness of God   38
  V. **What is God Like?**   41
    13. God is Holy   41
    14. God is Just   43
    15. God is Love   46
    16. God is Spirit   49
    17. God is Unlimited   51
    18. God is Perfect and Unchanging   54

Bible Activity Section   57

Introduction

Five thirty-seven P.M.: dinner begins—without Dad.

"Do I have to eat that?" asks 10-year-old Billy, pointing to his piece of liver.

"Yes—" Mother begins, only to be interrupted by a loud thump as Junior's plate lands up-side-down on the floor.

"Mom, do we have to have a family meeting tonight?!" asks sophisticated ninth grader, Becky. "I've got all kinds of homework; and besides; I'll miss my favorite TV program."

"You know what we've planned," says Mother looking up from the floor where she is helping Junior pick up his mashed potatoes. "We—" but again she's cut short, this time by the ring of the telephone.

"Yes?"

"Hon this is Jim. I have to work overtime. Won't be home till nine. Nothing I can do. Sorry."

Sound familiar? Plan your first family time and it seems nothing goes right.

We all *believe* in the family altar. Most of us have been encouraged to set aside a special time for the family. But when it comes to doing it—there are just so many obstacles that come up, so many activities to encroach upon our time. It's difficult to know how or where to begin.

The Family Hour Funbook is designed to meet these problems—to take the work and worry out of meeting with your family for a family hour with maximum participation, creativity and fun. Through a varied set of activities, including stories, Bible work, games, discussion times, role playing and "good time" experiences, it will enable your family to grow closer to each other and to God.

The Family Hour Funbook presents a variety of basic teaching information to help you formulate your children's understanding of who God is and how you can come to know Him better. The material is excellent for both children and teenagers, and it contains a unique Bible Activity Section that will excite each member of the family.

Why Have A Family Hour?

Moses said: "You must think constantly about these commandments I am giving you today. You must teach them to your children and talk about them when you are at home or out for a walk; at bedtime and the first thing in the morning. Tie them on your finger, wear them on your forehead, and write them on the doorposts of your house!" (Deuteronomy 6:6-8 TLB).

The Old Testament is filled with such commandments. God wants us to make His Word a part of our everyday lives. He has given all parents the privilege of training their children in His ways.

Many of us assume that it is the responsibility of our local church and the Sunday School department to make our children "see the light." But God gave that responsibility to us. The Bible makes it very plain that parents are to teach their own children.

Educators tell us that the home is far more important than any other educational experience a child receives. The training your children obtain from you (either purposely or by accident) comes in the most important school they will ever attend.

The time you spend with your children, on an organized level, helps to bridge the gap between what they're taught to believe and what they see practiced. It gives them an opportunity to interact with you on spiritual subjects. It lets them see you in an active role, openly declaring what you believe and why.

The establishment of a family hour can be a big help in keeping the lines of communication open between children and parents. Without such a regular period, it is easy for parents (or children) to become preoccupied with their own problems and concerns. The family hour helps all family members stop and take notice of what's going on in the lives of their closest relatives.

It is all too easy for Christian parents to unwittingly "innoculate" their children with Christianity by providing just enough of church and religious beliefs so that the children never "catch" the true faith. Christianity must be experienced before it becomes a life-changing reality; just talking about your beliefs isn't enough. The family hour provides an opportunity when both children and parents can experience their faith together in an open and honest way.

The Bible encourages Christian fellowship. But fellowship seldom seems to "happen." It often has to be "planned." The family hour provides a natural and easy climate to communicate on a spiritual level. It makes close, intimate, Christian fellowship possible and desirable.

The family hour provides creative stimulation to children and allows them to express themselves. It develops their confidence in their parents. It provides good experiences that will stand out in their minds for the rest of their lives. Done properly, the family hour is almost essential to a happy Christ-controlled family.

What The Family Hour Is Not

The family hour can provide many valuable spiritual experiences, but it must be remembered that it is not a cure-all for all family problems.

The family hour is certainly not an escape from practicing spiritual consistency on the part of parents. What you are often speaks louder than what you say. If you are inconsistent in your Christian attitudes and behavior—if you struggle with your own quiet time—if your personal Christianity is lethargic—no amount of preaching to your children one hour a week will convince them that Christianity works.

The family hour is not an escape from the integrity of practicing what you believe. Organized family devotions only have true value if you live out in your own life what you teach. The family time gives substance and structure to a young person's Christian "model." As he sees you live your relationship with Christ, and hears you explain what Christian faith is all about, he will grow to become "like Jesus" in the direct image of his human father or mother.

Family Hour Organization

Although a daily family altar has some advantages, most families will have difficulty maintaining such an active ministry. It is hard to get the children excited about a daily program because adequate parental preparation is almost impossible.

We highly recommend you plan your family hour on a weekly basis. This gives several advantages: You will have ample opportunity to plan and build exciting family experiences; the hour becomes special instead of routine; and each member of the family can be present because they will all know when and where it is to take place.

The family hour is not just a "souped-up" Bible lesson. It is a time when the family studies, shares, plays, and grows together. It should be a spiritual experience, but it should also be a total experience, allowing each member of the family input and output on his or her level.

This time cannot be compressed into half an hour. Ideally it should last two hours. Establish in your mind that games and activities are every bit as important to the spiritual growth of your children (especially young children) as is serious Bible study. We all learn best in an environment that is on our own level, so learn to structure your family time up or down to meet the needs of your own children.

The family hour should be organized like the family. Dad is in charge and should do most of the teaching. Mom is the vice-president and should also take an active role in the learning experience.

But don't feel you can't let the kids teach too. Often a high school or junior high teenager will be delighted to read the children's story or explain a lesson. If you put one of your children in charge, make certain you remember to praise him for doing the lesson.

A big problem which many families face is that they have several children on different levels. Every child has his own spiritual, emotional, maturity and interest level. Few activities will involve all of your children with the same enthusiasm.

That's why each lesson in this book provides a variety of different age and activity levels. Don't feel any compulsion to present the whole lesson. Each chapter is designed to provide material to meet the needs of the entire family. Select and use those portions which communicate the teaching message most effectively to your family.

An average family hour should consist of:
- Opening prayer
- The lesson
- Bible activities
- Family prayer and worship
- Fun activities

If you have both children and teenagers, you will want to present more of the material in each lesson so that all are reached fully. If the story or lesson is for a younger age, read it to everyone (the teens can handle it).

Assign different Bible activities for the older and younger family members, to be done at the same time. In this way you can look after each of your children and give them individual instructions. (It might be necessary for one parent to work with the younger ones, while the other works with the older ones.)

Make certain you prepare for each lesson. Know exactly what and how you will be presenting the lesson. Don't be tied to your notes. If you can present the material from memory, you will find you see better results.

Don't ask your children, "Which of these games do you want to play?" Say, "Now, we're going to play a fun game." Always communicate that you have prepared an exciting program and it will be difficult to squeeze all the fun in.

Establish your own program. Tailor the material in this book to meet your family's needs, depending on their age and interest levels. Remember, to keep them interested, do things they like. The fun activity should be something they want to do—not what you want.

Variety is important to the family—that's another reason why there are so many different types of activities in this book. Remember, however, that children—especially young children—need some regular structure so that they can form good habits. It is a smart idea to do some things the same way each week, like the opening prayer. Small children also enjoy hearing their favorite story over and over. They enjoy repeating the same role playing drama again and again. We all learn by repetition, but with younger children this is especially true.

The sections in this book that are enclosed in quotation marks are designed to be presented as dramatic material. We recommend that you familiarize yourself with this material so that you can present it from memory. If, however, you decide to read these sections, be certain you know the material well enough so you can read it with dramatic expression.

The secret of keeping your kids interested is being enthusiastic and excited yourself. When you read or tell a story, try hard to dramatize it. You can build interest by beginning next week's story and telling them you'll finish it at the next family hour.

Always stop activities at their peak. If you wait until everyone has lost interest in a game, no one will want to try it next time. Always keep them asking for more.

We trust that all of the activities in this book will be fun. But to avoid confusion, we have made a distinction between Bible activities and fun activities. Bible activities are those which are directly related to the Bible or the lessons in The Family Hour Funbook. Fun activities are those endeavors which have no teaching value and are simply designed to give the family good times together.

The Bible Activity Section, located at the end of this book, was created to get your children involved in meaningful written exercises. The materials are on different age levels, so you will have to decide which activities are suitable for your kids.

We recommend, especially for elementary-age children, that each child be given a large loose-leaf binder in which he can keep the various lessons, Bible studies and other Christian related activities for his growth. This notebook will make teaching easier for you, as review times can be accomplished easily. You'll also find that the children will receive a sense of completeness and accomplishment by keeping such a notebook.

It is also important that each of your children have his own Bible. If a child is too young to read, it is still a good idea for him to own his own New Testament (an inexpensive version will do) so that he can begin to sense the importance of God's Word.

You might want to give all your children a copy of The Way, the youth edition of The Living Bible. Many of the lessons in Getting to Know God use this modern paraphrase.

How To Begin

Because the family hour is a family project, you must first obtain the interest of each member of your household. If your children are young, you won't need their approval as they will easily accept whatever you want to do. But it is a good idea to build anticipation. Let them know that you are planning a special time just for them, but don't tell them anything; arouse their curiosity.

If you have junior high through college-age students, make certain you talk out your proposed plans with them before charging into the program. The obvious question they'll ask is, "Why are we starting this now? We never did it before!"

Don't be afraid to admit your own error for not starting earlier in their lives. Know why this is a good time to start the program now. If you've never had a family hour before, you must earn the right to have one now with this age group.

Talk about the communication problems every family faces. Give them an opportunity to come up with the idea of an evening set aside for the family. Let them know this will be their hour. Make them see how much fun it will be.

Notes To The Pastor

The Bible establishes two basic fellowship units: the Church and the family. Both "organizations" were designed to support each other. The stronger the family becomes, the more powerful the Church.

Your influence as Pastor can greatly aid parents in starting and maintaining a personal family hour in several ways: by setting a good personal example with your own family; by setting aside nights in the weekly church calendar when no activities will be planned; and by encouraging each family to become involved in their own program.

When a pastor and his church become involved in a weekly home program, it makes it easy for everyone to "give it a try." Your support and encouragement of the family hour will no doubt provide an unusual harvest of spiritual growth unlike any other program you can support.

I. Getting To Know God

Chapter One
Can You Know God?

YOUR PERSONAL PREPARATION

Introduction

We sometimes tend to think of God as Someone who lives "way out there"—Someone who is very big and important. And this is true. But we might also wonder how it could really be possible to know such a God personally.

God has made a way for us to know Himself and that is through His Son, Jesus Christ. Jesus said of Himself: "I am the Way—yes, and the Truth and the Life. No one can get to the Father except by means of me." (John 14:6, TLB).

Have you personally taken advantage of God's provision for getting to know Him? If not, you'll need to carefully read over and consider the material in chapters one and two. It will be difficult for you to communicate teachings that you haven't experienced. We therefore encourage you to begin a personal relationship with God by asking Jesus to come into your heart.

The purpose of lessons one and two is to introduce your family to God. If the members of your family unit already have a personal relationship with God, these lessons can serve as a valuable review of how one becomes a Christian.

If your family has never experienced this relationship with God, we encourage you to spend much time in prayer and preparation before giving these lessons. You want to make certain that you allow God to speak through you loudly and clearly. That can best be done when you know the material well and have spent adequate time in prayer for your own household.

Basic Bible Teachings

1. No man has seen God, but Jesus declares Him to us. John 1:18.
2. There is one mediator (one who gets two sides together) between God and man, and that's Jesus. 1 Timothy 2:5.
3. Although Jesus was in the form of God, He laid aside that glory and power so that He might become a man. Philippians 2:5-8.
4. God has a tremendous plan for each of us. John 10:10b; Jeremiah 29:11.
5. Jesus is the only way to God. John 14:6, Acts 4:12.

Lesson Objectives

1. That your children will learn Jesus became a man so that we could come to know God.
2. That your children will know the Bible reveals God to us.
3. That your family will discover God has a tremendous plan for each of us.
4. That your family will get excited about knowing God.

Things You'll Need

1. Three-by-five cards for writing down clues for "Who Am I?"
2. Scissors and paste for the "Keys to the Kingdom."
3. Several straws, small paper plates, balloons, and saltine crackers for "Indoor Olympics".

THE LESSON

Probe

The following PROBE questions are designed to help you introduce Getting to Know God. Your purpose here is not to get "correct" answers, but rather to make your family think. As they attempt to answer each question, you should respond with statements like, "That's close." "You're thinking!" etc. The point of PROBE is to build curiosity for what the coming lessons will teach.

1. "Does anyone know how big God is?"

(Answer: "There is no end to the universe—and God made the universe—so He must be as big as it is.")

2. "Can anyone tell me where God is now?"

(Answer: "Sure He is in heaven, but He's also somewhere else. Yes, He's everywhere at once! We'll talk more about that later.)

3. "How long has God existed?"

(Answer: "He's always existed. There never was a time when God didn't exist. He's always been alive, and He always will be. And next week we'll talk more about how we can get into God's 'Forever Family' so we can live forever just like Him.")

4. "Would you like to know God better?"

(Answer: "Well, next week we're going to talk about meeting God personally.")

Building Curiosity

"Next week I'm going to tell you a story about a fellow named Mike. He's just moved to a new neighborhood and doesn't have any friends. But Mike has a problem. He went into a store and . . . Well, I'd better not tell you anymore because that would spoil next week's story."

No matter how badly your children want to hear the rest of the story, let their curiosity grow.

"I can't finish telling you about Mike, but I'll tell you what I can do—Let's play a Bible game."

Who Am I?

Type or write the following clues on three-by-five cards. Make certain you number each clue because each one tells more about the subject. Pass out different clues to different members of the family. Let them trade clues when they want to.

As soon as someone thinks they know the Bible character, he should stand. Have the child whisper the name into your ear. If he is correct, he is the winner and sits to one side. If he is not correct, he is continues to look at clues. The game continues until everyone has guessed the correct answer or until the answer is given. Here are the clues:

1. I am no longer alive.
2. I lived during Bible times.
3. I am found in the New Testament.
4. I am a man.
5. I am a Jew.
6. I met Jesus.
7. I have a brother.
8. I am fairly quiet.
9. I used to fish for a living.
10. My brother talks a lot.

11. I introduced my brother to Jesus.
12. I am a disciple.
13. My father's name is Jonas.
14. My brother's name is Simon.
15. My name starts with the letter A.
16. There are six letters in my name.
17. ANSWER: My name is Andrew!

A Look in the Book

"We've just played 'Who Am I?' Now that we know that Andrew is our man, let's learn more about him." (Read John 1:35-41.)
1. "What was Andrew doing?"
2. "Who did he tell about Jesus?"
3. "What did he say about Jesus?"

"Now let's read John 12:20-22."
1. "What was happening?"
2. "Who told Andrew?"
3. "What did Andrew do?"
4. "What type of person was Andrew?"

(Answer: "He was the type of person who was always introducing people to Jesus.")

5. "Are you like Andrew? Do you help people meet God?"

Meeting God

"Have you ever wanted to meet and get to know somebody famous? How about the President of the United States? You could probably visit Washington D.C. and even tour the White House, but never even see the President. Why not?" (Let them suggest some reasons.)

"Of course, he's too busy to come out and meet you. But wait! Suppose you had a friend who knew the President well. Your friend knew exactly where and how to find the President and offered to introduce you. He would be a connection between you and the President, wouldn't he?

"You would follow your friend to the President's office, because he knows the way. As you both enter the door, the President would rise from his desk, shake your hand, and the two of you would begin to get acquainted. Afterwards, you would thank your friend, because without him it would have been impossible for you to meet the most important man in the world.

"In a sense, God is like the President of the United States. You can meet Him and get to know Him also. But you need a Friend to introduce you. Is that a problem? Not at all! You have a Friend who knows God personally. His name is Jesus. He is God's very own Son and He would like to introduce you.

"What do you think? Can you know God? (Wait for response.) How? (Wait for response.) Would you like to meet and get to know God? In our next family hour we'll find out how to arrange for that special introduction."

Keys to the Kingdom

In the Bible Activity Section there are several "Keys to the Kingdom." Cut the sheet containing these keys out of the book. Let each member of the family select a key and have him look up the Bible verse contained on it (or look it up for him if he's too young.) Once he has read the verse, let him cut his key out and paste it into his own notebook. Younger children might want to color the keys as well.

FAMILY FUN ACTIVITIES

Indoor Olympics

Have an indoor Olympics. Use the following events:
1. Javelin Throw—Throw a straw, then measure the distance.
2. Discus Throw—Toss a very small paper plate, then measure the distance.
3. Shot Put—Toss a balloon, then measure the distance.
4. 100-yard Dash—Eat two salty crackers and whistle.

Time each entrant giving a first, second and third place for each event. First place receives three points, second place receives two and third place, one. Total points at the end of your Olympics and crown your Champion. Be sure to have some kind of "crown" ready.

Chapter Two
Meeting God

YOUR PERSONAL PREPARATION

Introduction

In lesson one we learned it is possible to meet and know God, but that it must be done through His Son, Jesus Christ. But meeting God is just the initial step in coming to know Him. We don't know someone well at first meeting; knowledge about someone comes only when we spend time with that person. The same is true with God. Getting to know God takes time—a lifetime's worth of it. This book is only an introduction to God and what He is like for your family. Hopefully, each member of your household will want to learn and know more about our wonderful God as they progress through life.

This lesson points out that all of us have sinned. Because all have sinned, all must die. However, "The free gift of God is eternal life in Christ Jesus our Lord" (Romans 6:23b, NASB). Jesus died on the cross in our place. Through him we are united with God now and will live with Him forever.

Read over 1 John 5:11, 12. You can have the Son by simply receiving Him. A simple prayer—like the sample in the last part of this lesson—sincerely prayed, is the way you can introduce each member of your family to Jesus Christ as their own Savior.

If your children have not received Christ before, this could be the most important lesson you'll ever give them. Make certain you are adequately prepared to lead your children to Christ if they are ready to make that decision.

Basic Bible Teachings

1. God loves us. John 3:16.
2. God has very special plans for us. John 10:10b; Jeremiah 29:11.
3. All of us have sinned and fall short of God's glorious ideal. Romans 3:23.
4. The wages of sin is death. Romans 6:23.
5. Every man has to die because of sin. After that we all have to face God's judgment. Hebrews 9:27.
6. Even when we were sinners Jesus came to die for us. Romans 5:8.
7. Jesus took our sins on Himself, He suffered and died on our behalf. 1 Peter 2:22-24., 2 Corinthians 5:21.
8. Jesus wants to come into our lives and take control. Revelation 3:20; Romans 12:1, 2.
9. Salvation involves confession with our mouths that Jesus is Lord and believing in our hearts that God has raised Him from the dead. Romans 10:9, 10.

Lesson Objectives

1. That your family will understand what sin is and ask God for forgiveness.
2. That your family will want to meet God in a personal way through Jesus.
3. That your family will meet God.

Things You'll Need

1. For the section on the "Wolrdless Book," you will need to purchase several from your local Christian bookstore, or obtain the materials to make them: small sheets of construction paper in green, black, red, white and gold (or orange); glue and scissors.

2. For the tract entitled "God's Love," you will need a pair of scissors, a stapler and colored pencils or crayons to spruce up the illustrations.

THE LESSON

A Look in the Book

"Last week we found out that God wants to meet all of us. He's never too busy or too far away. He's always ready to come to us. In fact, God has some special things planned just for you.

"Let's look up John 10:10 in The Living Bible. The thief comes to kill and destroy us, but Jesus came to give us a happy and meaningful life."

1. "Who is the thief?" (Satan)
2. "Why does he want to kill and destroy us?"
3. "How does Jesus give us a full life?"

"Now let's look up Jeremiah 29:11-13 in The Living Bible."

1. "What kind of plans does the Lord have for us?"
2. "What will those plans give us?"
3. "How should we seek God?"

"Now read 1 John 4:9, 10 in The Living Bible."
"How much does God love us?"

"God loves us and wants to show us His wonderful plans on our behalf. But there is a problem. Let me tell you a story about a boy that will help to explain that problem."

Story Time

It was Mike's first day at his new school. Ever since his dad had come home with the news of his job transfer to another state, Mike had dreaded this day. All his life he had lived in the same neighborhood, gone to the same school, and had known everybody. But now, he had to start from scratch.

Mike arrived early and found his classroom. Nothing but strange faces glaring at him. The air seemed to whisper, "A new kid!" He really felt out-of-place.

"Who are you?" a tall boy asked.

At first Mike didn't know quite how to answer that simple question. Then he nervously replied, "Mike."

"Who?"

"Mike," he said louder.

"Oh, Mike! I thought you said 'Tike.'"

A group of girls nearby giggled. Deep inside, Mike resented that remark.

"You in this room?" asked the boy.

Mike nodded.

"That's neat," said the boy, matter-of-factly.

Mike found out later the boy's name was Derek. Derek was assigned by the teacher to be a buddy to Mike for his first day. At lunch time Derek told Mike he could sit with him and some other guys. At recess, when they chose teams, Derek talked the team captain into choosing Mike. Mike thought Derek must be a pretty nice guy to act like a friend to him when the teacher wasn't around. He discovered that Derek had a lot of friends, and these friends seemed to do whatever Derek wanted them to do.

The bell rang at 3:00 and everybody started home.

"You walking?" asked Derek, approaching with a boy named Scott.

"Yeah," said Mike.

"Which way?"

They were going the same way. Derek said Mike could walk with them.

A couple of blocks from school there was a liquor store. A lot of kids from school were standing around the door, drinking cokes and chewing gum. Derek began talking with two girls. Mike thought he must know everybody. It felt good to be friends with someone as popular as Derek; he would be an open door to many others.

"You got any money?" Derek asked, turning to Mike.

Mike had forty-five cents.

"Hey, loan me thirty cents, okay?"

"Sure," Mike replied, only too glad to be able to do something for his new friend.

"C'mon," said Derek. Mike followed Scott and Derek into the store.

There were several kids inside, looking at the counter, trying to decide what to buy. A few were at the cash register and the clerk was ringing up their purchases. The three boys went over to the pastry shelf. Derek was holding a can of coke he had picked up on the way in.

"Get something," he commanded.

"I don't have enough money left," said Mike. Derek and Scott looked at each other and grinned.

"So what?" said Scott, quickly grabbing a fruit pie and stuffing it into his coat pocket.

"See?" said Derek, glancing quickly at the busy clerk, then doing the same as Scott. "Who needs money when you can get a 'Five-finger-discount'? Now get something!"

Scott laughed and the two boys went to the counter. Derek bought his coke with the money he got from Mike, but neither of them took the pies out of their pockets.

Mike glared at the shelf. He knew that when he went outside, Derek and Scott would want to know if he took anything. If he didn't, they might call him a chicken. If he did, they would all have a big laugh and Mike would have won himself an important friend.

He felt a small trembling inside. He saw how easily it could be done. Not a very high price for friendship. Before thinking further, he snatched a pie and slipped it into his pocket. Smooth as silk, he sighed to himself, taking a breath of relief. The clerk was too busy to notice anything.

Having succeeded, Mike's nervousness was gone. Then a thought struck him. How would it look to the guys if I walked out with two? He stuffed one in his other pocket and made for the door. But before he could step outside . . .

"Wait a minute, young man," snapped the clerk. A rush like an electric current raced through his body. "Where d'you think you're going?"

"Out," Mike replied, trying to sound innocent. Outside, he saw Derek and Scott running off.

"Come here," ordered the clerk. Mike walked to the counter. "Empty out your pockets."

Mike pulled out the two fruit pies.

"You owe me fifty cents."

"I don't have any money," replied Mike, sheepishly.

"Fifty cents or I'm calling the police. I'm tired of you kids coming in here every day and ripping me off."

Mike thought of what it would mean to have to face the police and began to panic.

"Please, mister, don't do that! Honest, all I have is fifteen cents. Call my dad, okay? He'll pay you."

The clerk thought for a moment.

"All right. If your dad will come down here, I won't call the police. Here's the phone."

Mike hoped with all his heart that his dad would be home from work already. He was. And in ten minutes he was at the store.

The clerk explained what had happened. Mike's

dad apologized for his son and paid for the pies. The clerk accepted the apology, then turned to Mike.

"You're lucky, young man, to have a dad who cares enough about you to come down here like this and pay for what you took. It wouldn't have been the first time I called the police on a shoplifter."

Discussion Time

Ask these discussion questions:

"Who did Mike have to blame for the trouble he got into?"

(Answer: "Mike might blame Derek and Scott for encouraging him to steal, but really, he had no one to blame but himself. He had freely chosen to sin. Just because everyone else is doing something that is wrong, doesn't make it right.")

2. "What problem does Mike have, that we have too?"

(Answer: "Mike is a sinner. We are all sinners. Stealing is just one more proof that Mike had a sin problem.")

3. "What would have happened if Mike's father had not come down to the store?"

4. "Who is the hero of the story?"

(Answer: "Mike's father.")

Let's Think About It

"You know, you and I are in the same mess that Mike was in. 'But I didn't steal anything!' you might be thinking. Maybe not, but you have the same problem Mike has—you fall short. The Bible says, 'Yes, all have sinned, all fall short of God's glorious ideal.' That includes everyone of us. You and me and Mike and Derek and Scott. Everyone.

"When Mike stole from the store, Mike's dad had to come and pay for his crime. If his dad hadn't come, Mike would have faced punishment. In the same way, we need someone to step in and pay for our sins. Do you know who can do this? (Let them reply. Lead them to understand that God's Son Jesus Christ is the One.)

"Jesus paid for our sins by dying on the cross. He died in our place. He suffered like we should have suffered for all the sin we have done. When we trust Jesus to pay for our sins, we can start getting to know God, our heavenly Father, personally."

Making the Wordless Book

The Wordless Book describes how to be a Christian so that younger Children can understand. You can usually buy one at your local Christian book store. But it might be more fun (if you have the time during your family hour) to have your children make their own.

Buy small sheets of construction paper in green, black, red, white and gold (or orange). The book should measure about three inches tall and two inches wide. Make a pattern for each page that measures three-by-four inches. Once the children have cut each page out, have them fold the pages in half so they measure 3 inches by 2 inches.

Have the family glue one side of the gold page to the green cover. One side of the black page is glued to the back of the second gold sheet. The red pages are glued in next, followed by the white pages. When the book is finished, it should have a green cover; the first two pages will be gold, the next two are black, the next two are red, and the final two are white. Each page is glued to the next, and the white page is glued to the green cover.

Sharing the Wordless Book

Once the book is made, "read" it to your children (in your own words, of course).

"Inside our book we see two gold pages. Gold is the color of the streets of heaven. It reminds us of the glory of God. God wants us to meet Him; He wants us to come to heaven some day and live with Him—but there is this problem.

"The black page tells us about the problem. You know what it is. It is sin. Because we have sinned and fall short of God's glorious ideal, we cannot enter into heaven. This problem must be taken care of.

"The next pages show us how God took care of that problem. Red is the color of blood. Jesus shed His blood on the cross so that we might be cleansed of all our sin. And when He washes us from our sin . . . (turn the page).

"We become as white as snow. Do you want to have your sins forgiven? Do you want to be made pure and know God personally? It is the only way you can enter into God's 'Forever family.'

"All you have to do is invite Jesus to come into your heart and take control. Jesus said, 'Look! I have been standing at the door and I am constantly knocking. If anyone hears me calling him and opens the door, I will come in and fellowship with him and he with me.' " (Revelation 3:20, TLB).

At this point, each family member should be given the opportunity to receive Jesus into their lives, if they have never done so before. Receiving Christ is an individual matter, and should be done in the quiet of one's own heart. However, some may not exactly know how to do it.

Explain that we invite Jesus into our hearts through prayer. You may wish to lead in a simple prayer, having everyone repeat each phrase after you silently. Here is a suggested prayer:

"Father, I know that I'm a sinner. I know that Jesus paid for my sins. I want Jesus to come into my life and forgive my sins and help me be the person you want me to be. Thank you for forgiving my sins and answering my prayer. Amen."

For those who pray this prayer, emphasize that this is just the beginning of a wonderful and exciting Christian life.

God's Love

For teenagers, there is a tract entitled "God's Love," located in the Bible Activity Section. Have your children cut it out of the book, then fold, assemble and staple it. The tract will make an excellent tool to help you share the plan of salvation with your teenagers. Go through the booklet step-by-step and show how one becomes a Christian.

Have your children color in the illustrations in the tract. Also, this would be an excellent pamphlet for them to use in sharing the Gospel with their friends.

("God's Love" may be reproduced in limited numbers without written permission. It may not be offered for sale, however.)

FAMILY FUN ACTIVITIES
Fun With Riddles

Throw the following riddles at your family and see who can get the most answers correct. (You may want to get your own "Riddle Book" to supplement these.)

1. "How far can you go into a forest?" (Answer: "Only half-way. After that, you're coming out.")

2. "If a plane coming from England crashed right on the border between Germany and France, and the passengers were all from Italy, where would they bury the survivors?" (Answser: "They never bury survivors.")

3. "How can you tell if an elephant is in the bathtub with you?" (Answer: "By smelling the peanuts on his breath.")

4. "If a chicken could talk, what language would it speak?" (Answer: "Fowl language.")

5. "What did one wall say to the other?" (Answer: "I'll meet you at the corner.")

6. "How long is a piece of string?" (Answer: "Twice as long as from the middle to one end.")

7. "If you have two common American coins that add up to 30 cents, and one of them is not a nickel—what are the coins?" (Answer: "A quarter and a nickel. The quarter, of course is *not* a nickel."

II. Getting To Know God Better
Chapter Three
Listening To God

YOUR PERSONAL PREPARATION
Introduction

Those of us in this country are privileged to live at a time and in a place where we have liberal access to the Scriptures. Yet so often we take the Bible for granted and are negligent in studying it. The Bible itself exhorts us to responsibly utilize God's Word (See 2 Timothy 2:15).

The purpose of this chapter is to teach the importance of Bible study and that it can really be enjoyable. Urge each member of the family to make Bible study a daily habit. Although this is not a "how to" approach to Bible study, some guidelines and suggestions are given. As a parent, you will want to demonstrate the important role Bible study plays in your life.

Basic Bible Teaching

1. God's Word is eternal. Isaiah 40:8.
2. God's Word is faithful. Psalm 119:160; Proverbs 30:5.
3. God's Word is spiritual food. Matthew 4:4.
4. God's Word is a weapon of spiritual warfare. Ephesians 6:17; Hebrews 4:12.
5. God's Word is worthy of constant examination. Psalm 119:11; Acts 17:11.
6. God's Word develops character qualities. Romans 15:4; 2 Timothy 3:15-17.

7. Purity is achieved through God's Word. Psalm 119:9-11.

8. Joy is found through reading God's Word. Psalm 119:16, 162.

9. Guidance is given by God's Word. Psalm 119:105.

10. Blessing is derived from obedience to God's Word. James 1:25; Luke 11:28.

Lesson Objectives

1. That your family will understand how important God's Word is in getting to know God.

2. That your family will become excited about the Bible.

3. That your family will start listening to what God is saying in His Word.

Things You'll Need

1. You'll need a chalkboard or some other erasable surface for "Memorize a Verse."

2. In the Family Fun Activity Section you will need a wastebasket, a wadded up piece of paper, a paper target, a needle and thread. Also, a typical family parlor game like Monopoly, Scrabble, Rook, etc. should be used.

THE LESSON

Story Time

"Samuel Morse was born back in 1791, fifteen years after the birth of our nation, in Charleston, Massachusetts. After graduating from Yale University, he studied painting.

"But Morse hadn't yet discovered his true calling. He also had an interest in telegraphy, and realized that since sounds, but not voices, could be carried by electricity through wires, a code was needed. So in 1832, long before the invention of the telephone, he developed an excellent code to be used in sending messages over telegraph wires. This code was to be known as the Morse Code. It spread like wildfire across the country, and it wasn't long before people were sending and receiving Morse Code messages all across the nation.

"Morse Code is still used today. It is made up of a combination of dashes and dots. Each letter of the alphabet is represented by a different combination. Since 'E' is the most frequently used letter, Morse gave it the shortest sound—a single dot; and since 'T' is the next most frequently used letter, he gave it a single dash. Coded letters are thus strung together to spell words. You may use Morse Code as a 'sound' code by using a code oscillator (which gives a series of 'beeps'), or you can use it as a 'sight' code by using flags or flashing lights.

"Sam Morse felt that his code could be learned in a very short period of time. He was not trying to make a secret code, but one that could be used easily by many people."

Learning the Morse Code

In the Bible Activity Section is a page of messages written in Morse Code. A key to the code is also given so that your children can decipher the Bible messages. Have them cut out the cards and have each person decode a verse.

The Bible: God's Message to Us

"God wants us to know what a wonderful life He has planned for us. This is why He gave us the Bible. It contains everything we need to live a happy Christian life.

" 'Now wait a minute,' you say, 'I've tried to read the Bible but it just doesn't make sense.'

"There are several things you need to know, if this has been true for you in the past. The Bible is not really just one book, it is a collection of books, and as such, it shouldn't be read from front to back anymore than you would read a dictionary from A to Z. It wasn't meant to be read that way.

"If the Bible seems old and stale, you should try a more contemporary translation like The Way (youth edition of The Living Bible). Also, we must ask God, the Holy Spirit, to help us 'decode' the more difficult passages each time we read the Bible.

"Acts 17:11 tells us of a group of Christians who searched the Scriptures daily to learn how to live. This is God's purpose for giving us His Word. Today, we are more fortunate than they were then, because we can each have our very own copy of the Scriptures. This makes it easy to read and study God's Word anytime.

"This is not true everywhere in the world. I want to read you a true story about a man who spent thirteen years in a Communist prison just because he was a devout Christian."

The Importance of God's Word

The following excerpts are taken from Tortured for His Faith, by Haralan Popov, and are used by permission. It is an excellent book for your family to read together. It will make you stop and think about how you take your freedom and your Christianity for granted.

"One day I noticed that Stoil, the man whose bed was next to mine, had something in his hands. I couldn't tell what it was, but it looked like a little book. Then I saw what he was doing. Stoil was tearing a page out of the book in which to roll a cigarette. To my astonishment I saw that it was a New Testament!

"I had not seen a Scripture portion for five years! Instinctively I grabbed it from Stoil and looked at it. Stoil started to grab it back as tears flowed down my cheeks. He stopped, caught with surprise at what it obviously meant to me.

"'Stoil,' I asked, Where did you get this book?'

"'When we were transferred here from the first barracks area. I found it in a trash can.'

"I said, 'Stoil, please give me the book.'

"'No,' he answered firmly, 'I'm reading it.' He grabbed it from my hands.

"But I knew he wanted the thin paper only for use as cigarette paper! I couldn't bear the thought of God's Word, which I had not seen for five years, being used as cigarette paper.

"'Stoil, I will give you all the money I have for the book.' At this particular time we were able to keep a little money on hand at times to buy from the prison canteen.

"When I offered Stoil all the money I had, his eyes widened. Then he brightened and answered: 'Pastor, since you want it so much you may have it. Here, take it!' Then I held it! God's Word! I wept before the men and they turned their heads so as not to embarrass me.

"For five years I had starved physically, but I had starved even more spiritually, and I can tell you the spiritual hunger is more painful than the physical . . .

"What an indescribable loss it is to be without a Bible or Testament! During my whole time in prison I felt an emptiness and sharp, almost physical pain at being denied the Word of God. I had, of course, read God's Word my whole Christian life, and knew verses and longer portions, but because of the torture and beatings I had been through and the long time I had been separated from God's Word, I had forgotten certain parts. Strangely, torture often has the effect of clouding the memory. I noticed this effect very often.

"I knew I wouldn't be able to keep the New Testament for long. Eventually the prison guards would find and destroy it. But as long as I remained here on the island I could hide it out in the fields, in the straw and hay. Each day I hid it in a different place so they wouldn't notice a pattern. After hiding it in straw and hay I began to dig holes, put up a marker of some kind and dig it up to read. By all means, I knew I had to keep it in the fields because our cells were often searched. But since my best chance to read it was late at night in my cell, I took the risk of taking it back to the cell with me, praying all the while there would be no surprise inspection that night. This also gave me more opportunities to read to the prisoners.

"Realizing I wouldn't have the Testament for long, I decided to memorize as much of it as possible. Everywhere I went I had the Testament with me. I always found occasion to study it. First, I memorized 1 Peter, then Ephesians, 1 John, the Gospel of John, Romans 1, 5 and 8, 1 Corinthians 13 and 14, and 2 Corinthians 5. Forty-seven chapters in all.

"When I was later moved to a regular prison, it was impossible to hide the Testament any longer. But by then I was almost a 'walking New Testament.' Now with God's Word I began greatly to enlarge my ministry to my fellow prisoners. During the years ahead, God prospered my ministry in prison as I used every possible opportunity to minister to the men about me."

Preaching by Prison Telegraph

"In prison we had developed a 'Prison Telegraph.' One existed in most prisons because in prisons, communication with one another is very important. This was the way prisoners passed news along the 'prison grapevine.' The prison telegraph consisted of a crude 'Morse code.' One tap on the wall stood for the letter 'A'. Two taps were 'B'. Three taps were 'C' and so on, all the way through the alphabet. To say something with the letter 'V' in it took ages! Yet, it worked.

"Left alone, I had an idea. If the Prison Telegraph could be used to spread rumors and news, why couldn't it be used to spread the Gospel? I took my tin drinking cup and began tapping on the wall and waited. Sure enough, in just a few moments, there came a tapping sound from the other side.

" 'What is your name?' I tapped.

" 'M-I-T-S-H-E-V' he replied.

" 'How long have you been there?' I tapped.

" 'Three weeks,' he tapped back.

"I soon developed a special 'technique' for tapping. If it were discovered by the guards, I would be stopped. So, I stood up in the cell with my back leaning on the cell wall, as if I were resting and tapped with the cup in my hand behind me. This way I could keep my eye on the Judas-hole and immediately stop if I heard or saw the little door over the Judas-hole open. I told Mitshev to listen because I had something very important to tell him.

"He tapped back that he was ready."

"I asked him if he were a born-again believer in Christ. 'No', he replied.

" 'Have you heard that Christ died for our sins?'

" 'Only in the Orthodox Church when I was a boy,' Mitshev replied.

" 'Listen,' I tapped, 'because I want to tell you what Christ can do for you.'

"Then, for the next three days, interrupted only by sleep, I 'preached' a message of God's love and Christs' salvation to Mitshev. After we stopped for a night, Mitshev would start by tapping, a question such as, 'But, Pastor, how can my sins be gone? I don't understand.' This was good! Mitshev was thinking.

"On the fourth day, Mitshev tapped back, 'I am ready now to believe in Jesus, pray for me. I am ready to accept Christ.' I told him to get on his knees in his cell and I would get on mine in my cell and we would pray together. A few minutes later, Mitshev tapped back. 'I do thank God. I have given my life to Him.' After his conversion, I built his faith for three more days until I was taken back to my regular cell. All of this was by tapping with a tin cup. Not one audible word was ever said.

"I never saw Mitshev, but I knew he had found Christ."

Memorize a Verse

"Committing a Bible verse to memory can be challenging and rewarding. Memorizing means learning to say verses by heart. David said to God, in Psalm 119:11, 'I have thought much about your words, and stored them in my heart so that they would hold me back from sin' " (TLB).

Write Isaiah 40:8 on a blackboard or some other erasable surface. The first player reads the verse from the board. If he reads it correctly, he erases one word (of his choice). Each reference counts as one word.

The next player reads the verse, inserting the missing word as he does so. If he can do it correctly, he too can remove a word. This continues until the entire verse is erased. If a player reads the verse incorrectly, he may not erase a word. By the end of the game, all players should be able to quote the verse by memory.

A Look in the Book

In the Bible Activity Section there are several Bible studies that your teenagers can do. These "Sing Alongs" are taken from the Youth Bible Study Notebook published by Tyndale House. Have one team study Psalm 119:12-20 while another studies Psalm 119:101-106. If you have several older teens, you might want to purchase copies of the entire book for them to use in their personal Bible study time.

Daily Bible Reading

Have each member of your family clip out one of the "I Read My Bible!" slips in the Bible Activity Section. Have them paste the slips in their notebooks so that they can keep track of whether or not they read the Bible every day. Announce that everyone who reads the Bible daily will receive a treat at next week's family hour time.

FAMILY FUN ACTIVITIES

Free-Throw Contest

Wad up a piece of paper and have a "free-throw contest." Select a likely wastebasket and have the family line up at an appropriate distance. Give each member five chances at a close distance. Hooks, left-hand shots, long shots, etc. can be added to make the competition more interesting. Keep a record of their success, and establish the family free-throw expert.

Mini-Target Practice

A needle with some thread tied into it makes an effective dart for target practice. Test out several different needles along with different lengths of thread before beginning this contest. On a piece of construction paper, draw a simple target which can be taped (with masking tape) to a door or maybe even the back of a padded chair. Keep score and determine who the winner is.

Family Game

Select a favorite family game and play it. Good selections would be Monopoly, Risk, Checkers, Scrabble, etc.

Chapter Four
Prayer: Talking To God

YOUR PERSONAL PREPARATION

Introduction

Getting to know God better involves spending time talking with Him. The way we speak to God is through prayer, and let's face it, if you don't spend much time talking to someone, you don't have much of a relationship with them. The same is true with God: if you want to know Him better, spend more time talking with Him.

Prayer is very important to every Christian's personal walk with God. The Bible exhorts us (Philippians 4:6), and Jesus teaches us by example (Mark 1:35), to pray faithfully. When spiritual difficulties arise in our lives, we can often attribute them to a lack of prayer on our part.

We cannot overemphasize the importance of prayer to the spiritual life of your family. You will want to encourage them to a regular prayer life-style. The most effective way you can do this is by setting the example yourself and giving them a model to follow.

Your family should pray together—at meals, before bedtime, when important decisions need to be made—anytime when it is appropriate to the situation. Younger children can watch, or you can pray outloud a few words at a time and they can repeat after you. It is important to make prayer a part of your daily routine.

Prayer is a wonderful experience and an adventure with God. Be sure to depend on God's power, unleashed through your prayer, as you lead your family spiritually. Prayer can make the difference between frustration and joy for your Christian family.

Basic Bible Teaching

1. Prayer is how we talk to God. Philippians 4:6.
2. God promises to hear our prayers. 1 John 5:14.
3. God promises to answer our prayers. 1 John 5:15.
4. If we have sin in our hearts, we short-circuit our own prayers. Psalm 66:18.
5. Confession is how we cleanse our sins. 1 John 1:9.
6. God wants us to pray hard. James 5:16; Luke 18:1-8.
7. God does not want us to repeat the same words over and over. Matthew 6:7.
8. God wants us to intercede for our Christian friends. James 5:16; Colossians 4:2-4.
9. God wants us to pray for non-Christians, that they might be saved. 1 Timothy 2:1-4.
10. God wants us to pray for our governmental rulers. 1 Timothy 2:2.
11. God wants us to pray for workers to reach the harvest of non-Christians. Matthew 9:37, 38.
12. God calls the prayers of His children incense. Revelation 5:8.

Lesson Objectives

1. That each member of the family will understand the importance of prayer.
2. That your family will look forward to talking to God.
3. That your family will begin to talk to God on a daily basis.

Things You'll Need

For the "Family Fun Activities," you'll need a newspaper and several pairs of scissors.

THE LESSON

Story Time

"It's a dark desert night on the two-lane interstate highway. You and your family are driving to a distant vacation resort. All that can be seen are the reaching headlight beams of an occasional vehicle rushing past.

"Suddenly, mysteriously, the beams of an approaching car begin to wander. They are nearing rapidly, and become steadily aimed at you. Apparently, the driver has lost control and you must avoid him! Failure to do so would mean a horrible crash and probably instant death.

"But there's no time to think—you must act quickly. You are on a high-speed collision course, and panic is beginning to seize you. Frantically, desperately, you slam on the brakes and jerk your car off onto the shoulder of the road. But the sudden change in direction is too great, and the car loses its balance and overturns onto the shoulder of the road.

"You can't see much of anything. Everyone is pressed against the crushed top of the car, which is upside down in the dirt. You manage to free yourself and crawl out an open window. The rest of your family is trapped inside the car and you need help—fast!

"The desert highway is black: no lights, no people, no hope. The car that caused the accident is nowhere in sight—apparently still swerving down the road. Then, as welcome as a morning sunrise, a pair of headlight beams appear on the horizon. The vehicle steadily approaches, though to you it seems to take forever.

"You wave your hands over your head furiously in an effort to flag it down. The vehicle, a pickup truck, slows to a halt. You run to the window to explain the emergency, but before you can say anything, the perceptive driver is talking into the microphone of his CB radio, calling for help. Instantaneously, radio waves are carrying the message for miles through thin air to a nearby town. Help is on the way!

"Within the hour, rescue operations of fireman and paramedics have freed your family from the wrecked car, and given them emergency medical treatment on that deserted highway. Had it not been for speedy communication by CB radio to someone who could help, your family might not have been saved!

"In another place and time, a man named Peter is arrested on false charges and thrown into prison without bail and with no hope of a trial. Rumor has it that the authorities plan to execute him in a few days.

"A few nights later, in another part of town, Peter's friends are meeting together in a house, praying for his release. They know that God is hearing their prayers and that He can do anything.

"Suddenly, the prayer meeting is interrupted by a knock on the door. A girl named Rhoda goes to answer it, but before she can open the door, she hears Peter's voice outside. She is so happy that she immediately turns and runs back into the room.

" 'Peter is out in the street and he's free!' she exclaims.

" 'You're crazy, Peter is in jail.'

" 'But I heard with with my own ears!' she insists.

" 'Are you sure, Rhoda?'

" 'Positive!'

" 'Then they must have killed him already,' someone suggests, 'and it was his ghost you heard.'

"But Peter started banging on the door again, and when they opened it, they discovered the Apostle, standing there in the flesh—alive! They hugged Peter and shouted for joy!

" 'How did you get out, Peter?'

" 'It was a miracle from God!' he tells them. 'I was sleeping, double-chained between two guards, when an angel slapped me on the side and woke me up.'

" 'Quick, Peter,' he said, 'get up!'

" 'Then the chains fell off my wrists and I got up and got dressed. The angel led me out of the prison past sleeping guards and through wide open gates, and then led me here!' God had heard the prayers of Peter's friends and rescued him!

"The first story I told you was made up, but the second actually happened (Acts 12:1-17). CB radio has come a long way since Thomas A. Edison invented the first wireless telegraph way back in 1883. It has been used to save many lives. But an even more amazing invention came years earlier by the greatest Inventor of all time—God. That invention was prayer."

Discussion Time

1. "Why do you think prayer is more amazing than CB radio?"

(Discuss, for instance, that prayer: (1) transmits further, (2) can be done with no equipment and without any licenses, (3) that it communicates instantly, and (4) puts us in touch with God, the greatest source of help and power).

2. "How often do you think God wants us to pray?"

(Make certain you know what the Bible says on this point).

3. "What types of things does God want us to pray for?"

(Again, know what the Bible says on this. Be sure to emphasize that God is concerned that we bring those things which are on our hearts. In other words, He wants to hear about those little things that are of interest to us.)

Daily Prayer

Have each member of the family clip out one of the "I Prayed Today!" slips in the Bible Activity Section. Have them paste it into their notebooks so that they can keep track of whether or not they pray everyday. Announce that everyone who prays daily (on their own) for the next week will receive a treat at next week's family hour time. (Make certain that you treat anyone who has completed his or her Bible reading for last week.)

What's Your Handle?

"What's your handle? Every CB operator has a

handle. A handle is a label by which he is known when talking on the air. If you had a 'prayer handle,' what would it be? How would you like to be known by God, when you pray?"

Work on some Christian handles for each member of the family. A handle might be Prayin' Paul or Praisin' Peter or High Rising Henry, etc.

Personal Prayer

You will want to do your best to investigate a regular time of prayer for your family. Several of the older children might be ready for a help like the Personal Prayer Notebook, written by John Souter and available from Tyndale House Publishers.

Family Prayer Time

"God knew that we would need to talk to Him often, so He made prayer simple. And He wants us to pray every day. In fact, He wants us to stay in an attitude of prayer all the time (See 1 Thessalonians 5:17).

"Prayer is easy—it's just like talking to a friend. You don't have to worry about saying things just right, because God knows what you mean (See 1 Samuel 16:7; Romans 8:26, 27). And God wants us to pray not only when we need help, but for other reasons, too. He wants us to thank Him for things He has done for us, and to tell Him how much we love Him.

"What are some of the things we can be thankful for? (Give your family the opportunity to think of all the things for which they should be thankful.)

"Let's talk to God now, one at a time, around the circle; and let's tell God what we have just told each other. Let's tell Him how thankful we are for all He's done. (Encourage each member of the family to say something to God, however small it may be. Make certain they know how important it is to God that they talk to Him.)

"Now, let's discuss together the needs we have as a family. (Discuss such things as illness, the salvation of a friend or relative, a school problem, etc. Let everyone talk freely.)

"Okay, let's talk to God again, this time telling Him about our needs. Each of us should tell God about those things which are on our hearts."

FAMILY FUN ACTIVITIES

Newspaper Race

For each participating member of your family, tape the corner of one page of the local newspaper to one wall of the living room. Each person is to use a pair of scissors to cut his newspaper into one long piece (with a zig-zag cut) so that it stretches across to the opposite living room wall. The first person to do this without breaking the paper or pulling off the taped end wins. If the outcome is close, try it a second time.

The Missing Dollar

"Three men spent a night in a hotel. When they were ready to check out they found their bill was thirty dollars—ten dollars each. They gave the money to the bellboy to take it to the desk. When he paid the cashier, he found that the hotel was refunding five dollars to the men. So the bellboy kept two dollars as a tip and returned one dollar each to the three men. That made each man pay nine dollars. Three times nine is twenty-seven. Add this to the two dollars retained by the bellboy and you have twenty-nine dollars. Where did the other dollar go?"

The answer: The catch is that the men paid twenty-five to the hotel and two to the bellboy—that totals at twenty-seven. The three dollars that was refunded to them makes thirty.

Chapter Five
Fellowship: Enjoying God Together

YOUR PERSONAL PREPARATION

Introduction

One of the best ways to get to know God better is through Christian fellowship. Some claim that they can worship God as well at home as they can at church—so why go to church?

This is really not completely true. They may worship well at home, for a while. But soon, without the warmth, love and encouragement of other Christians (Hebrews 10:24, 25), they will grow cold in their Christian commitment. Have you ever seen a hot charcoal fall away from the rest of the coals in a fire? Which coal goes cold first? Without the combined heat of the others, one coal hasn't got a chance.

Fellowship is an essential ingredient in our growth as Christians. In a society where we are constantly being bombarded by Satan's lies, we need others to build us up in the faith. Your family should therefore have a regular place of fellowship to attend.

Fellowship, however, does not have to be within the walls of a church structure—it can happen anywhere two or more Christians are gathered together. True fellowship usually doesn't just happen; we usually have to plan the time to enjoy God together.

As you begin to prepare yourself for this week's family hour, concentrate on learning what fellowship is and how you can create an atmosphere that will allow your entire family to become involved in a worshipful experience.

Basic Bible Teachings
1. Fellowship is communion with God. 1 John 1:3.
2. Fellowship is also communion with men on a spiritual level. 1 John 1:3.
3. Fellowship involves stimulating one another to love and to do good deeds. Hebrews 10:24.
4. Fellowship involves spending time together. Hebrews 10:25; Acts 2:42, 46.
5. Fellowship involves a special sense of God's presence when two or more believers gather in Christ's name. Matthew 18:20.
6. Fellowship involves a close relationship with other believers and easily happens when people live and eat together. Acts 2:46.
7. Fellowship involves praising God. Acts 2:47.

Lesson Objectives
1. That your entire family will come to understand what fellowship is all about.
2. That your family will *want* to experience true fellowship with each other and with God.
3. That your family *will* experience rich fellowship during the family hour.

Things You'll Need
1. For the "Object Lesson" you will need a single piece of paper and a thick telephone book.
2. For "Christian Comics" you'll need several appropriate comic strips out of your local newspaper. White out the words with Liquid Paper. A photocopy may be easier to write on.
3. For "Family Praise Game," you'll need several small pieces of paper and a pencil for everyone.
4. For the "I Game," in the Family Fun Activities section, you will need ten beans for each member of the family and a winner's (token) prize.
5. For the "Joke Time," in the Family Fun Activities section, it would probably be wise to buy a good joke book. There are several, edited by Bob Phillips, that are good: The World's Greatest Collection of Clean Jokes, More Good Clean Jokes, The Last of the Good Clean Joke Books, and The All American Joke Book.

THE LESSON

Object Lesson

"Do you know what the word 'fellowship' means? (Let them respond.) A good way to remember what it means is by thinking of 'fellows in a ship.' They are together in calm and stormy seas. They cannot separate without leaving the ship. And as long as they are together, they can navigate the ship much better than each could alone.

"In this way, churches are like ships: they need a crew that is really together in order to run things properly. This is part of what 'fellowship' means. It is a body of believers who meet together to worship and love the Lord together.

"How do believers strengthen each other in fellowship? I have two objects here to show you how: one is a piece of paper, and the other is a large telephone book. This piece of paper is very simple to rip in half (have someone demonstrate). But when many pieces of paper are bound together as in this telephone book, it is almost impossible to rip them in half (have someone try).

"The same is true of Christians. You and I, alone, are like a single piece of paper—we are only so strong. But when we fellowship together with other Christians, we are much stronger. Let's read Ecclesiastes 4:9-12 (in The Living Bible).

"The Bible tells us that the members of the early Church were bound together, just like this telephone book. It says: 'They joined with the other believers in regular attendance at the apostles' teaching sessions and at the Communion services and prayer meetings.' (Acts 2:42, TLB)."

A Look in the Book

Read Acts 2:40-47 in The Living Bible. Have the

family help you make a list of all the ways that the early Church practiced fellowship together.

Once you have your list, have the family members discuss what each activity is and how it's done. Have them check off each activity that your family can do at home together.

Learning to Praise God

Praise is involved in the fellowship process. Spend a few moments talking about what it means to praise someone. You can praise what they have done or what they are.

Talk about all the things God has done for us: creation, salvation, forgiveness of our sins, daily food, etc. Then discuss what God is like: Holy, loving, completely truthful, etc.

Tell your family that you are going to praise God. As Psalm 150:6 says: "Let everything that has breath praise the Lord" (NASB). You want to thank and praise God as a family for who He is and what He's done.

Christian Comics

Before you begin the family hour, cut comic strips out of the daily paper. Cut off the dialogue or white it out with Liquid Paper so that your family can write in Christian words.

Be careful to make selections in which the pictures will lend themselves to becoming Christian. Instruct your family to add dialogue that talks on the theme of fellowship.

The Importance of Church

"The Lord wants us to attend church for two important reasons: to worship and praise Him, and to build each other up in the faith. David said, 'Hallelujah! I want to express publicly before his people my heartfelt thanks to God for his mighty miracles. All who are thankful should ponder them with me' (Psalms 111:1, TLB).

"What miracles has God done for us that we should praise Him for? (Let them respond, being sure they realize that salvation is a miracle.)

"Another way of worshiping the Lord is hearing His Word. He has given us wise teachers to make the Word of God easier to understand. God is pleased when we delight in His Word (See Psalm 119:16).

"But how are we supposed to build each other up in the faith? (By loving each other.) You know how good you feel when someone does you a favor or says something nice to you. This is what God's love is like. Loving each other is a sign that we know God. (See 1 John 4:7-9.)

Read Hebrews 10:24, 25. "See how important going to church is? It makes us stronger Christians and helps us to get to know God even better. Let's thank God for our church and ask Him to help us love each other more."

Sermon Search

This activity can be used more often during the year if desired. It is a good idea to do this periodically so that the family will be more responsive to the sermons they hear each week. Assign one or two of these activities each Sunday, then double check on the complete assignment at the next family hour.

1. Illustrate the sermon with a picture or design.
2. Remember (and write down) the main point of the sermon.
3. What part of the sermon did you like best?
4. What part of the sermon didn't you understand?
5. What did the sermon tell you to do?

Crossword Puzzle

In the Bible Activity Section you will find a crossword puzzle for older members of the family. The puzzle uses verses on fellowship, and you may wish to work it through for—and with—your younger children. The puzzle is based on the New American Standard Bible; so to avoid confusion, that translation should be used to answer the questions.

Family Praise Game

Learning to find the good in another person and to praise it is an important part of fellowship. Have one member of the family leave the room. While he is gone, each family member writes down something about that person for which they can praise God. One person collects all of the pieces of paper before the family member returns to the room.

Upon his return, the praises are read, one at a time. He tries to guess who wrote each praise. Redistribute paper to the family again as another person exits. Continue this game until everyone has had an opportunity to be praised.

FAMILY FUN ACTIVITIES

The 'I' Game

This activity can show the family how often they refer to themselves. Before dinner, give each member of the family ten beans (or some similar small object). The point of this game is to keep all your beans and get some from the other members of the family. You lose a bean every time you use the word "I." If you're talking with someone else and they say "I," you will get one of their beans. The person who has the most beans by the end of dinner is the winner.

Family Joke Time

Have a family joke time in which every member of the household gets an opportunity to tell a joke, in turn. Make certain that everyone knows that the family tells only clean and wholesome jokes. Also, tell everyone to get in a "laughing mood" so that they will be good listeners as well as tellers.

You probably won't be able to keep this joke time going very long without the aid of a good joke book or two. Several good selections are mentioned under the "Things You'll Need" section.

III. People Who Knew God

Chapter Six

Abraham Trusted God

YOUR PERSONAL PREPARATION

Introduction

One of the best ways to get to know God is to look at the lives of godly men. The Bible is full of such men whose lives give us a further glimpse of what our God is like. This is the first of three lessons that deal with Bible personalities.

Abraham is a unique character in that he is given many titles: "father of the faithful," "friend of God," "father of them that believe," to name a few. His name literally means "father of a multitude."

Abraham is a picture to us of God the Father. Just as Abraham loved God enough to be willing to sacrifice his son Isaac, so God loved us enough to send His Son to die for our sins (John 3:16).

Abraham is used throughout the New Testament as an example of faith. To really get to know God well we must learn to trust Him just like Abraham did. As you teach this lesson, concentrate on the fact that God is worthy of our trust and faith.

This week's lesson can best be illustrated by taking the family for a walk. Most of the activities are designed to be given out-of-doors. Be certain you familiarize yourself with the story in Genesis 22:1-18 and the rest of the material in this chapter. Also, make certain that you leave home with all of the different objects you'll need to complete this lesson at the park.

Basic Bible Teaching

1. Without faith it is impossible to please God. Hebrews 11:6.
2. Faith is the "evidence" of the things we hope for. Hebrews 11:1.
3. Faith is the "substance" of things we have never seen. Hebrews 11:1.
4. Jesus made it plain that we are blessed when we believe in Him without having seen Him. John 20:29.
5. We are to live by faith. Romans 1:17.
6. Abraham was counted righteous because he trusted God at His Word. Romans 4:3, 18-24.

Lesson Objectives

1. That your family will appreciate a great Bible character: Abraham.
2. That your family will understand how important faith is to God.
3. That your family will begin to exercise their faith in God.

Things You'll Need

1. The Living Bible for "A Look in the Book."
2. Some paper and pencils for the "Abraham Acrostic."
3. Blindfolds for the "Faith Walk."
4. Softball equipment for the "Family Fun Activity."

THE LESSON

Story Time

Tell the family that you are all going for a drive, then a short walk. Don't tell them why or where. If possible, go some place where there are few distractions—like a nature park. In your own words, tell the story of Abraham and Isaac after you begin walking along. Pause occasionally to emphasize a point. Use your imagination and creativity here and there to captivate their interest.

You may wish to relate the story in this fashion, based on The Living Bible:

"Abraham was a man who lived 4000 years ago, far away in the land of Canaan. He knew God very well.

"One day, God spoke to Abraham.

" 'Yes, Lord?' replied Abraham.

" 'Take your only son, Isaac, whom you love very much, and go to the land of Moriah and sacrifice him there as a burnt offering upon the mountain that I will show you.'

"This command from God must have really startled Abraham. Could the Lord actually want him to kill his son? After all, hadn't God made him wait twenty-five years to have him. And now, he was well over 100 years old! But, nevertheless, Abraham was sure that God knew what He was doing, and he obeyed.

"The next morning Abraham got up early, chopped some wood for the fire, saddled his donkey, took his son Isaac and two servants, and started off to the place God had told him to go. After three days Abraham could see the place at a distance.

" 'Stay here with the donkey,' Abraham told his servants, 'and my son and I will travel yonder and worship God, and then come right back.'

"Abraham placed the firewood on Isaac's shoulders, while he himself carried the knife and flint for starting the fire.

"Now Isaac didn't know that the Lord had spoken to his father and had commanded him to sacrifice him on the altar. He thought that they were going to sacrifice a lamb for the Lord as was the custom.

" 'Father,' Isaac asked, 'we have the wood and the flint to make a fire, but where is the lamb for the sacrifice?'

" 'God will take care of that, son,' Abraham replied.

"When they arrived at the place where God had told Abraham to go, he built an altar and arranged the wood for a fire. Then he tied up Isaac and laid him on the altar over the wood. Abraham took the knife and raised it up to plunge it into his son, to kill him!

"Suddenly, an angel shouted to him from heaven, 'Abraham! Abraham!'

" 'Yes, Lord!' he answered.

" 'Lay down the knife and don't hurt the boy,' the angel said, 'because now I know that God is first in your life—you were willing even to give up your beloved son!'

"Then Abraham noticed a ram caught by his horns in a bush. So he took the ram and sacrificed it, instead of his son, as a burnt offering upon the altar. Abraham called that place 'The Lord Provides'—and it still goes by that name today.

"The angel called again to Abraham and said, on behalf of the Lord, 'Since you have obeyed me and have not even held your son back from me, I will bless you unbelievably and multiply your descendants into countless thousands and millions, like the stars in the sky and the sands along the seashore. They will conquer their enemies and be a blessing to all the nations of the earth—all because you have obeyed me.'

"So you see, by being willing to give his one son to God, Abraham was to gain an uncountable number of descendants. The Jewish people today are the descendants of Abraham. Also, every Christian is a spiritual descendant of this man of faith.

"God doesn't ask us to give up something big very often, like He did with Abraham. But He does often ask us to give up little things. Usually, these are things that we want to do but know we shouldn't. We should give these things to God and trust Him, like Abraham did, so that He can give us something far better in their place. It may not come right away—it didn't for Abraham—but we can trust God that it will come!"

Discussion Time

Sit down and discuss what Abraham did.

1. "Did it take a lot of faith on Abraham's part to be willing to sacrifice his son?"

2. "What would you have done in his place?"

3. "Do you think he thought God would actually allow him to kill his son?"

4. "Why does faith please God?"

5. "What about Isaac? Did he have faith in his father and in God?"

6. "How did God reward Abraham for his trust and faith?"

A Look in the Book

Look up Hebrews 11:1 and 11:6. Have the family members look at these two verses and discuss the importance of faith.

To complete your Bible study time, read Romans 4:18-25 in The Living Bible. The passage discusses

Abraham's faith and how he was an example to us so that we should trust God like he did.

Abraham Acrostic

On several slips of paper write Abraham's name down the left side, one letter under the other. Have the family members come up with a sentence or slogan for each letter of his name that tells us about Him. For example, the "A" could begin the statement "Always trusted God." "B" might begin "Beloved of God." And so on.

A Faith Walk

To teach the family members more about what faith and trust really is, have a faith walk. Blindfold half of the family. Each member of the "seeing half" leads a blindfolded person over and around rough terrain, "by faith." Instruct each member to hold the hand of the person they are guiding and to describe what each step will enounter. This simple activity will help build our trust in one another. Make certain everyone has an opportunity to go on the walk.

FAMILY FUN ACTIVITIES

Softball Game

While you are at the park, pull out the softball equipment and play some games. Most families don't have enough for a "real game," so play some of the other softball activities.

Try "Three Flies Up." Someone bats and the rest field. When a fielder catches three flies, he bats. If you drop a fly, it subtracts one from your score, however.

Try "500." Someone bats, like in Three Flies Up. Only this time, points are kept. If you catch a fly, it's worth 100 points. Catch the ball on one bounce and get 75; on two bounces, and get 50; and on three, you receive 25. No points are awarded if the ball bounces four or more times. If you drop any of the above, subtract the same number of points from your score. If you want to make the game a little more difficult (for older teenagers), specify that you cannot go over 500 points. If you have 475 points, you must catch a three bounce grounder or you will go over. If you go over, you lose all your points.

Advertising Slogans

While you are driving home, think of different advertising slogans and apply them to God. For example: "Jesus is the real thing," or "You're in the Jesus Generation," or "God Satisfies." Have your family members keep count of the number of Christian advertising slogans you can make up using secular jingles, etc.

Chapter Seven
Daniel Prayed

YOUR PERSONAL PREPARATION

Introduction

In an earlier lesson we took a look at the subject of prayer and how important it is as a means of getting to know God. In this lesson we will see how prayer was a reality in the life of one of God's choice servants.

Daniel's intimate relationship with God was largely due to the high priority prayer had in his life. In the twentieth century it is often easy for us to lose sight of the fact that our prayers are a powerful part of our relationship with God.

Prayer is the power by which things come to pass which otherwise would not happen. Our faith is the power by which it is decided how much of God's will shall be accomplished through us. Once God reveals what He is willing to do for us, it is our responsibility to pray to make it happen.

First John 5:14, 15 gives us the assurance that if we pray in God's will He will hear and answer. We must realize that this is a promise from God of spiritual power and results. Let's not sell the prayer-process short. God wants to give us results—but He can't if we don't pray.

God has graciously provided us with human examples like Daniel to follow. You may be having difficulty making prayer a daily part of your spiritual exercise. Admittedly, prayer is often hard, and there are really no shortcuts or gimmicks for us to use. But for Daniel, devotion to prayer carried a high price. The familiar story below (from Daniel 6) illustrates how well Daniel knew God through prayer—and how well we can know Him.

Basic Bible Teaching

1. Prayer can accomplish great works. John 14:12-14; 16:24.

2. God is able to give us much more than we ask for. Ephesians 3:20.

3. The Lord loves to hear our prayers. Proverbs 15:8.

4. God answers the prayers of ordinary type people. James 5:16-18.

5. God answers the prayers of those who believe He will answer. James 1:5, 6.

6. God answers prayer. Psalm 65:2; 66:19, 20.

7. Not only does God hear our prayers that are in His will, but He answers them. 1 John 5:14, 15.

Lesson Objectives

1. That the family will learn that prayer is one of the major ways a Christian keeps a close relationship with God.

2. That the power of prayer will be emphasized.

3. That each member of the family will *want* to talk to God daily.

4. That each member of the family *will* talk to God daily.

Things You'll Need

1. Paper on which you will put simple abstract marks for the "Story Squiggles."

2. For the "Bean Race" you will need a bowl full of navy beans and several straws.

THE LESSON

Story Time

"Daniel was a young man who lived thousands of years ago in the city of Jerusalem in Judah. He was a tall, handsome man who always carried a happy expression on his face. People must have wondered what he was so happy about. Listen closely to the following true story, and see if you can figure out the reason.

"Daniel was about 15 years old when his homeland was attacked by the Babylonians. They brought many things back to Babylon with them, including Daniel and some of his friends.

"The king of Babylon picked Daniel and his friends (who were all part of the royal family of Judah) to be his advisors. He could tell they were all strong, healthy, smart and sensible. The king put them in a three-year training school to teach them the Chaldean language and literature. When they graduated, they did become the king's advisors. But Daniel was the king's favorite because of his tremendous abilities.

"Years later, there was a new king in Babylon—a man named Darius. By this time, Daniel had worked himself up to the position of president. There were three presidents in the land, and these three were second in authority only to the king.

"King Darius, however, saw that Daniel was much more capable than the other two presidents, and he began to think about putting Daniel in charge of the whole kingdom since he himself was getting to be an old man.

"Well, of course, this made the other presidents very jealous, so they got together with some of the other officials in the kingdom to see if they could find some fault in Daniel to tell the king about. But as hard as they tried, they couldn't find anything wrong with him.

" 'What about his faith in God?' someone suggested. 'Maybe we can get Daniel in trouble because of that!'

"The others smiled in agreement. Daniel's faith in God was their only chance. So they thought up an evil scheme and went before the King.

"'King Darius, live forever,' they greeted. 'We have all decided that it might be a good idea for you, the king, to make a law that for thirty days, anyone who asks a favor of God or man—except from you, your Majesty—shall be thrown into the lion's den. Sign here, your Majesty, and the law cannot be removed.'

"King Darius, being old and feeble-minded, took this as a compliment and signed the law.

"Daniel had been in the habit of going up to his bedroom, three times a day, kneeling down and praying to God. He would thank Him for all the wonderful things He had done; then he would share his needs. Prayer was the secret to Daniel's success. It was through prayer that Daniel came to know God as a personal friend. And God responded to this friendship by making Daniel successful.

"When the law passed, Daniel knew about it. He also knew that anyone who broke the law would be thrown into the lions' den to be eaten alive. But Daniel knew his relationship with God was much more important than any law men could come up with; so he kept on praying, three times a day!

"So the men responsible for the law gathered at Daniel's house and found him praying to God. Quickly, they ran to the king, and reminded him of the law.

" 'Didn't you sign a law,' they asked, 'that says

whoever asks favors from anyone except you for thirty days shall be thrown into the lions' den?'

" 'Yes,' replied the king, 'I signed that law, and it cannot be taken back.'

"They all looked at one another and grinned.

" 'Well,' they said, 'that fellow Daniel is paying no attention to your law. He is up in his room right now praying to God. He does this three times a day.'

"When the king heard this, he became very angry with himself. He had forgotten all about Daniel, who served God, when he signed the law. He spent the rest of the day trying to think of a way to save his trusted friend, but he couldn't come up with any way out of the dilemma. The law could not be erased.

"That evening the men returned to the king.

" 'Your Majesty,' they said respectfully, 'there is nothing you can do.'

"The king realized, unfortunately, that they were right. So he ordered Daniel to be arrested. But before he was thrown into the lions' den, the king said, 'Daniel I hope the God whom you worship will save you.'

"Then they threw him in. What a high price Daniel had to pay for prayer! But he knew God so well that he wasn't afraid of what men could do to him."

Discussion Time

Stop right here in your story and talk about the importance of paying the price. Let each member of the family participate and agree that it pays to follow God. Let them also talk about the fact that it pays to pray. Then build their curiosity:

"Do you have any idea how the king felt about having to send Daniel into the lions' den? I'll tell you all about how the king felt and what happened to Daniel—next week!"

Let the family members insist upon hearing the whole story now. You can be "persuaded" to tell them how the king felt and what happened to Daniel.

Story Time [Continued]

"The King was so depressed that he went to bed without dinner, but he could not sleep all night. The next morning, the king hurried to the lions' den, opened the door, and called, 'Daniel, servant of the Living God! Was your God, whom you pray to, able to save you from the lions?'

"Then he heard Daniel's voice. 'Your Majesty, live forever! My God has sent an angel to close the lions' mouths so they can't touch me, because I am innocent before God and I haven't wronged you!'

"The king was insane with joy! He had Daniel removed from the lions' den and not a scratch was found on him because, the Bible says, he believed in God.

"See how important prayer is? Daniel got to know God so well through prayer that he was willing to die for Him! We said at the beginning of the story that Daniel walked around with a happy look on his face. Can you figure out why?" (Discuss as a family how knowing God brings joy inside that cannot be hidden.)

Story Squiggles

Make a few "Story Squiggles." Draw simple squiggles on several sheets of paper. These abstract marks are to be used as the basis for drawings about Daniel's experiences. Have each family member select a squiggle and use it as a part of his drawing about some part of the story of Daniel in the lions' den. Compare and talk about their drawings.

Courtroom Trial

For the older children, this is a good "thinking" activity. Divide the family into two sides. One side attempts to prosecute Daniel for not obeying the king's law, the othe side defends Daniel against his accusers.

Have the two groups cut out their "Trial Briefs" from the Bible Activity Section. Daniel's enemies will receive the "Trial Brief for the Prosecution" while his friends will receive the "Trial Brief for the Defense." Give each side about ten minutes to prepare their cases, and then have the trial.

Telegram to God

Have the family prepare a telegram to God which explains how they feel about Him. Instruct them to make it full of worship and praise.

Use the "Western Telegram" form in the Bible Activity Section to record the final form of this prayer.

Conversational Prayer

Begin the conversational prayer time by saying that the family is going to "transmit" their telegram to God.

"Prayer is conversation with God. We can talk to Him, together, just like we talk together as a family. We don't even have to close our eyes."

When you send your telegram you might want to have the family keep their eyes open for a change. The main reason Christians close their eyes when praying is to keep from being distracted. We do not have to keep them closed and a change of pace can be extremely stimulating to your family prayer time.

FAMILY FUN ACTIVITIES

Bean Race

Fill a bowl full of dried navy beans. Each member of the family is given a straw. They are to suck through it and pick up beans (one at a time) and place them in another container. Hold the beans in place by sucking and placing the tip of your tongue on the end of the straw. Any beans dropped between the bowl and the goal container don't count. Each family member gets the same amount of time (if you have smaller children, you might want to give them extra time to make things even). Keep track of each one's points.

Number Games

1. Have someone select a number without telling you what it is. You'll figure it out. Suppose the number they select is 15. Here are the instructions you'll give him:

Number selected	15
Double it	30
Add 1	31
Multiply by 5	155
Add 5	160
Multiply by 10	1600

"What is the result?" you ask. He should say "1600." In your mind eliminate the two zeroes and subtract one which leaves you with 15. That was his original number. Tell him his number was 15.

2. Here's another number game to try when the first one gets old. Tell someone to think of a number (perhaps their age). Double it, then add five, and multiply by 50. Add the change in your pocket. Subtract 365 days in the year and add 115. Their first number or age will be the first two digits, their change will be the last two.

Let's say their age is	13
Multiply by 2	26
Add 5	31
Multiply by 50	1550
He adds the change in his pocket (26 cents)	1576
Subtract 365 days	1211
Add 115	1326
He is 13 years old and has	26 cents

Chapter Eight
Paul Gave His All

YOUR PERSONAL PREPARATION

Introduction

Probably no one, next to Christ Himself, was more responsible for the spread of Christianity than was the apostle Paul. The fascinating biography of this colorful character is more interesting than fiction.

Paul's life of sacrifice is a challenge to each one of us in our service to the Lord. Perhaps this is because Paul believed "For to me, to live is Christ, and to die is gain" (Philippians 1:21, NASB).

Paul is a good example of a man who came to know God better because he gave more of himself to the Lord. It is usually true that you only get back in relationship to how you give out. Proverbs says: "He who waters will himself be watered." (Proverbs 11:25b, NASB).

You will want to communicate Paul's life-style, in this lesson, as an example of a man who knew God well. Paul is a real person whom each one of us can follow and imitate. (See Philippians 3:17.)

Basic Bible Teaching

1. Paul's education: Philippians 3:5; Acts 22:3; 23:6; 26:4, 5; Galatians 1:14.
2. His citizenship: Acts 16:37-39; 22:25-28.
3. His persecution of Christians: Acts 7:57-8:3; 9:1, 2; 22:4, 5; 26:9-11; 1 Timothy 1:13.
4. His conversion: Acts 9:1-20; 22:3-21; 26:2-23.
5. His early Christian life: Acts 9:17-30; 11:22-30; Galatians 1:15-20.
6. His first missionary journey: Acts 13:1—14:28; Galatians 1:21-24.
7. His second missionary journey: Acts 15:36—18:22.
8. His third missionary journey: Acts 18:23—21:16.

9. His trial and imprisonment at Rome: Acts 21:17—28:31.

Lesson Objectives

1. That your family might get to know a man (Paul) who knew God well.
2. That your family might become excited about giving their all to God.
3. That each member of the family might give his all to God.

Things You'll Need

For the "Family Fun Activity" you will need to select several good Christian biographies for your family to read. Make certain you have several on hand. There are some suggestions given in that section of this chapter.

THE LESSON

Story Time

Have one of the older members read this story about the apostle Paul. You might want to give him an opportunity to practice reading it ahead of time so that he can do a good job.

"Paul was a great man who lived near the time of the Lord Jesus. But if you were to meet him walking down the street, you probably wouldn't think much of him. Paul was a very small man, in fact, his name really means 'little.' He was partly bald, with a hooked nose and eyes that did not provide him with good vision. Yet, in a real sense, Paul was a big man because he had a big heart for God, whom he knew personally.

"The story of Paul is an amazing one, but true. He was born a Pharisee Jew in the city of Tarsus, and his father was a Roman. As a boy, he studied hard in the Jewish religion, memorizing Scriptures and learning Jewish history. His father contributed to his well-rounded upbringing by teaching him the trade of tentmaking.

"As a young adult, Paul studied under the great philosopher Gamaliel. This training sharpened his mind, but he obtained even greater knowledge from 'the school of experience.'

"Paul understood and loved the Jewish faith. To him, there was nothing in the world more important. This feeling was so strong that it drove him to hate Christians, who were telling everyone that Jesus from Nazareth had risen from the dead. These people infuriated Paul because they claimed that the Ten Commandments were not enough anymore. He was determined to stamp them out—even if it meant murder!

"One day while Paul was walking to the city of Damascus, to arrest some Christians, a bright light from the sky fell upon him. It was so bright that he fell to the ground. Then a voice spoke.

" 'Paul! Paul! Why are you persecuting me?'

" 'Who is speaking, sir?'

" 'I am Jesus, the one you are persecuting. Now get up and go into the city and await my further instructions!'

"What could Paul do but obey? But the light had blinded him and he could not see. The men who were with him had heard the voice but they hadn't seen the light. They led him into the city where he did not eat or drink for three days. Finally, his sight returned when God sent a Christian to him.

"Paul had met Jesus Christ, and he knew he would never be the same. He was to learn later just how much this experience was going to change his life!

"Paul knew that God had some special plans for him. He spent the next ten years studying the Scriptures and praying to God in preparation for the Lord's work.

"The rest of Paul's life was spent as a missionary to the Gentiles in Asia Minor and Europe. He made three separate missionary journeys, bringing the good news of Jesus to people and founding churches in several major cities. He was also responsible for writing 13 of the 27 books in the New Testament.

"But these accomplishments did not come without great pain. While referring to his opponents, he tells us of some of his experiences in 2 Corinthians 11:23-27:

" 'They say they serve Christ? But I have served him far more! (Have I gone mad to boast like this?) I have worked harder, been put in jail oftener, been whipped times without number, and faced death again and again and again.

" 'Five different times the Jews gave me their terrible thirty-nine lashes. Three times I was beaten with rods. Once I was stoned. Three times I was shipwrecked. Once I was in the open sea all night and the whole next day. I have traveled many weary miles and have been often in great danger from flooded rivers, from robbers, and from my own people, the Jews, as well as from the hands of the Gentiles.

" 'I have faced grave dangers from mobs in the cities, from death in the deserts, from storms on the seas and from men who claim to be brothers in Christ but are not. I have lived with weariness and pain and sleepless nights. Often I have been hungry and thirsty and have gone without food; often I have shivered with cold, without enough clothing to keep me warm' (TLB).

"Paul came face-to-face with death many times while serving Christ. He sacrificed many of the comforts of the world for God. To this, Paul says:

" 'Yes, everything else is worthless when compared with the priceless gain of knowing Christ Jesus my Lord. I have put aside all else, counting it worth less than nothing, in order that I can have Christ . . .' (Philippians 3:8, TLB).

Application/Prayer

"We can see that 'Paul gave his all' to God. But what about us? Are we willing to pay the price Paul paid to serve the Lord? Are we even willing to risk our friendships with non-Christians?

"Let's pray right now and ask the Lord to give us willing hearts to do whatever He asks us to do, and to help us to get to know Him better."

Man Hunt!

For the older children there is a "Man Hunt!" Bible study form in the Bible Activity Section. This method is taken from the Youth Bible Study Notebook by John Souter, published by Tyndale House. This study deals with a search for facts on the apostle Paul's life.

Character Slogans

The title of this chapter is "Paul Gave His All." The family may enjoy thinking of character qualities that rhyme with their names. Some examples are:

"Dan Is God's Man"
"Diane Does All She Can"
"Bill Is in God's Will"
"Sue Asks God What to Do"
"Jim Lives for Him"

With these slogans, colorful posters may be designed using colored pencils, crayons, etc. Each child can hang their poster in their room as a reminder of a goal they can work toward.

Business Cards

In the Bible Activity Section there are a number of "Business Cards" designed to impress upon the members of your family the importance and excitement of being God's man or woman. As your family cuts out these cards and fills in their names and character slogans (from above), emphasize how important it is to "give our all" to God.

FAMILY FUN ACTIVITY

Reading Time

Select for the family a number of good Christian books that they can begin to read during this part of the evening. Here are a few suggestions:

FOR YOUNGER CHILDREN

Some People, by Mary Carlson. Tyndale House Publishers.

Spire Christian Comics by Al Hartley. Revell Publishers.

FOR ELEMENTARY AGE

Ivan and the Hidden Bible by Myrna Grant. Tyndale House Publishers.

Ivan and the Secret in the Suitcase by Myrna Grant. Tyndale House Publishers.

I'm Out to Change My World by Ann Kiemel. Impact Books.

FOR TEENAGERS

The Pleasure Seller by Bruce Danzara. Tyndale House Publishers.

Tortured for His Faith by Haralan Popov. Zondervan.

The Hiding Place by Corrie ten Boom. Various publishers.

Pearl by Donita Dyer. Tyndale House Publishers.

IV. Who Is God?

Chapter Nine

God the Father

YOUR PERSONAL PREPARATION

Introduction

Some Christians struggle with the Fatherhood of God. They don't like to think of God as Father, because they identify Him with the problems they have faced with their earthly fathers.

The Christian family is perhaps the best school a child can attend in which to see his heavenly Father revealed. Certainly no earthly father is perfect, but the Bible uses him as an illustration of the way in which God treats His children. God, we're told, will correct and discipline us just like human fathers do (read Hebrews 12:7-10). God will give good gifts to His children just like our earthly fathers do (see Luke 11:11-13).

A child will usually respond to his heavenly Father in direct proportion to his relationship with his earthly father. You cannot teach this in one lesson—you must behave, on a daily basis, like God the Father behaves toward His children.

If your children see you as a heavy-handed authority figure, if they think of you as inconsistent, or feel that you don't love them; this lesson will be hard for you to teach effectively. You may have to begin by admitting that you have not been the kind of father that God wants you to be. If this is true, it will be hard to admit, but this is what you will have to do to begin to correct the situation.

As you teach this lesson, try to communicate not so much the doctrine of God the Father as you do His personality, His love, and His provision for His children.

Basic Bible Teaching

1. The Father created everything. 1 Corinthians 8:6.
2. The Father knows our needs. Matthew 6:8, 32.
3. The Father meets our needs. Matthew 6:33.
4. The Father loves us. John 3:16; 16:27.
5. The Father is merciful. Luke 6:36.
6. The Father loves the Son. John 3:35; 5:20.
7. The Father is one with the Son. John 14:8, 9; 10:30.
8. The Father sent the Son. John 3:17.
9. The Father sent the Holy Spirit. John 14:26.

Lesson Objectives

1. That the family will understand that God is a loving Father.
2. That the family will come to understand they are in God's family.
3. That the family will learn to trust in God and His wisdom.

Things You'll Need

1. For "Styrofoam Art," you will need a styrofoam cup for each member of the family.
2. For "My Two Fathers," you will need several old magazines (with lots of pictures of people), scissors, glue and construction paper.
3. For "Psalm 23 Pantomimed," it would be wise to use some props which suggest what the story is all about. For example: a shepherd's stick, shawl for the shepherd, oil, etc.
4. For "Quiet Time," the young children might want to color some pictures of our Shepherd, so have some colors and paper ready for them.
5. For the "Family Fun Activities," have either a game of Pit or Checkers available.

THE LESSON

Story Time

"A man and his wife stroll past a row of newborn babies in a ward of a large hospital. They have waited years for this day. At last the time has come to adopt a child for their very own. This is the day and there is an important decision to make.

"The nurse directs them to the baby that is available for adoption. Their eyes fall upon the child and instantly they agree—this is the one. Their love for a helpless baby is born. They will love him as if he were their own flesh and blood.

"In the days to come, an important decision must be made. A first name must be chosen for the child and, of course, he will share the last name of his new parents.

"Once home, the baby will be given everything he needs by his loving parents. He will be fed good food, have his diapers changed regularly and be given warm clothes to wear. The child will mature into a young man and eventually will inherit all his parents own. All of this is possible because his new parents love him."

Application

"Did you know, as a Christian, you are like the child in this story? That's right! Your heavenly Father has adopted you into His forever family. You belong to Him and can depend on Him for everything.

"The first thing He did was choose you to be His child. This is a special privilege, and you had no more to do with His decision than the baby did in the hospital.

"Do you think God chose us because we're all so good looking?" (No, I don't think all of us would make it, if that's how He made His decision.)

"Do you think God chose us because we're all such good people?" (Nope! That can't be it!)

"Maybe God chose us because we're so smart." (No, we wouldn't all make it again!)

"God chose us because He wanted to. And there's nothing we did to deserve it.

"Because He chose you, your heavenly Father has a unique love for you. Because He loves you, God will provide everything you need—on that you can always depend.

" 'Long ago, even before he made the world, God chose us to be his very own, through what Christ would do for us; he decided then to make us holy in his eyes, without a single fault—we who stand before Him covered with his love. His unchanging plan has always been to adopt us into his own family by sending Jesus Christ to die for us. And he did this because he wanted to!' (Ephesians 1:4, 5, TLB).

"Finally, your heavenly Father wants you to grow up into a mature Christian. He has given you the Bible as your spiritual food. He takes care of you by forgiving your sins that you commit every day. He has even provided spiritual (character) 'clothes' to protect you from Satan.

"We will all meet God the Father face-to-face someday. At that time, you will inherit all the riches that are His, and you will live with Him forever. I can hardly wait to see Him! What about you?!"

Styrofoam Art

This activity may seem difficult, but once the wheels of creativity begin to roll, fascinating and insightful truths will arrive.

Each person is given a styrofoam cup. Allow five minutes for everyone to fashion his cup into some shape or form that will illustrate his relationship to his Heavenly Father: past, present, or future. He may break it, poke holes in it, leave it whole, or whatever he wishes to do to it.

If the group is desperately stuck for ideas, make some suggestions to help them out. Breaking the cup into pieces could represent one's life outside the will of the Father; a crown could represent one's inheritance from the Father; or a heart could symbolize the Father's love. Encourage originality.

Afterwards, have each person show his creation to the group and explain its meaning.

My Two Fathers

Supply the family with several old magazines, scissors, glue and construction paper. (Make certain the magazines have lots of pictures of people.) Have each member of the family cut out pictures which tell a story about his two fathers. Each story should have a caption (which may be written out for the younger children) or the children can explain what each picture means to the group when everyone is done.

Psalm 23 Pantomimed

Divide the family into two teams. Each team will pantomime (act out without words) the message of Psalm 23. It might be a good idea to provide some props which can be used to help tell the story. For example: a shepherd's stick, shawl, oil, etc.

Have one team act out the first verse; the other team will act out the second, and so on until all the verses have been portrayed. You can read each verse slowly while the team acts out the words.

Once the Psalm has been completed. Discuss how it is an example of our heavenly Father's love and concern for us.

Quiet Time

Have the family spend ten minutes of "Quiet Time" talking to our heavenly Father. Older members of the family may want to meditate on a verse or two in Psalm 23. Younger children may want to color a picture of our Shepherd. Each member of the family should give himself wholeheartedly to this time with God. It will be exciting to see each member talking to God on his own.

FAMILY FUN ACTIVITIES

Play Pit

If you have four or more members in your family, a good change-of-pace game is Pit. Buy a set of cards and have a ball. Your kids will love it.

Checkers Championship

With a set of checkers, have a "checkers championship." Everybody plays one game with everyone else. Keep track of the winners and the person with the best win-loss record wins the championship. If you don't have two sets and you want the championship to move faster, make a temporary set using buttons or coins and a makeshift board. Also, if you have smaller children who can't play as well, have older players start with two or three less checkers.

Chapter Ten
God the Son

YOUR PERSONAL PREPARATION

Introduction

To fully understand the work of the Father, we must understand about His Son, Jesus Christ. We can have no insight into God's nature without realizing the significance of His sending His only Son into a world destined to reject Him. In fact, it is impossible to know the Father except through His Son.

It is important that your children realize that Jesus is "God the Son." It is a mistake to think of Him as any less God than the Father. They are one in essence and purpose, differing only in their ministry and personhood.

While the lesson material in this week's family hour time does not emphasize the deity of Christ, it would be well for you to remind your family that Jesus is both our Savior and our God.

Basic Bible Teaching

1. Jesus existed before He became a man. John 1:1-3; 8:56-59.
2. The Bible expressly calls Christ "God." John 1:1; 20:28; Titus 2:13; Hebrews 1:8; 2 Peter 1:1; 1 John 5:20.
3. Jesus has the perogatives of God. He forgives sin: Luke 7:47, 48. He will raise the dead: John 5:25-29. He will execute judgment: John 5:22, 27.
4. The Bible gives to Christ the works of God. He creates: John 1:3; Colossians 1:16. He upholds: Colossians 1:17; Hebrews 1:3.
5. Jesus accepted worship. Matthew 14:33; 15:25; 28:9, 17.
6. Jesus is given titles that teach his deity. Immanuel (God with us), Matthew 1:22, 23; I Am, John 8:58; etc.
7. Jesus came to die for us. John 3:16; Philippians 2:5-8.

Lesson Objectives

1. That the family will realize Jesus is God in the flesh.
2. That the family will understand how important the Son's ministry is to our salvation.
3. That the family will want to spend time becoming like Jesus.

Things You'll Need

1. For the "Story Script: 'The Landowner's Son,'" you might want to develop props to make the story easier to dramatize.
2. For "The Parable Frieze," you will need a long roll of butcher or shelf paper and colored felt pens.
3. For "Scrambled Words," you'll need to print two verses on several pieces of paper so they may be scrambled.
4. For the "Family Fun Activities," you will need either modeling clay or finger paints.

THE LESSON

Story Script: "The Landowner's Son"

The following drama, based upon Luke 20:9-16, is to be read together as a family, with each reader having his own part. Depending upon the size of your group, you may wish to assign more than one part to each person, or take turns reading a part.

For older family members you may want to use the story as a play script, to be acted out. You may do this informally, or more elaborately by using props, costumes and well-rehearsed lines. The play could even be put on for friends or for the rest of the family at a later time.

CHARACTERS:
- ELI: The landowner.
- MICAH: The first messenger.
- NATHAN: The second messenger.
- AMOS: The third messenger.
- ACHAN: The evil boss of the farm.
- JESHUA: The landowner's son.
- NARRATOR

NARRATOR: Many years ago, there lived an old man named Eli who had a good wife, several married daughters and one son named Jeshua. Eli was an honest and sincere man who had spent his life making good investments. In his old age, he was a wealthy man owning land everywhere. One day, Eli called in Micah, one of his assistants.

ELI: It's time for the harvest at the farm in Erets. The farmers out there are bringing in the new crop. They will keep their share as payment for their work, but you take a crew and collect my share.

MICAH: Yes sir. I will carry out your orders.

NARRATOR: So Micah gathered his crew with wagons and donkeys, and set out for the journey to the land of Erets. After several days they arrived at

the point overlooking the fertile valley owned by Eli. The crops looked healthy and luscious.
MICAH: Wait here for me. I will talk to Achan alone.
NARRATOR: Micah rode his donkey down to the farm alone. Achan greeted Micah with a scowl.
ACHAN: So you've come again to steal from our harvest! I've been expecting you!
MICAH: How can a man steal what is already his?
ACHAN: Who breaks his back working these fields? Whose sweat has made this soil rich? Not Eli! (Several strong-armed farmers come and stand by Achan.) Tell him if he wants his share to come and get it himself. Now get lost!
MICAH: I have orders to return with his portion of the harvest.
ACHAN: Okay, men! Let's send Eli the fruit of his labor!
NARRATOR: Achan gave the farmers a nod, and they beat Micah up. They laid his limp body on his donkey and slapped it off in the direction it came from. Micah's crew received him, cared for his wounds, and carried him back to Eli.
ELI: Those farmers are hard and wicked men! But I will give them another chance. Nathan, I'm going to send you to bring back my share. You know the danger of this assignment and what happened to Micah.
NATHAN: Yes sir! You are a fair man. It is not right for them to defy you! I will do my best!
ELI: Thank you Nathan, I know you will.
NARRATOR: Days later, Nathan arrived with his crew at the fields. He too preferred to go down alone to talk with Achan.
ACHAN: Did Eli get my message?
NATHAN: Yes. He learned that you and your men are more wicked than he had thought. You know that part of the harvest is rightfully his! He has sent me to give you another chance.
ACHAN: (Laughing out loud.) Another chance! How nice of him. Our answer is the same. Now go back the way you came!
NATHAN: Not without what I came for!
ACHAN: Yes. It would be a shame to send you back with nothing, having come all this way. (Motions to his men.) Take care of our guest.
NARRATOR: Nathan tried to defend himself against the attack of the farmers, but there were too many of them. Soon, he fell to the ground.
  When Eli heard the news, he was furious. Not to mention insulted. But his anger was cooled. He knew that anger would not get him his share of the harvest.
ELI: No one must ever say that Eli is unreasonable or unfair. I will send one more messenger to appeal to them. Perhaps, after a third time, they will listen.
NARRATOR: So Eli called Amos, the best of his men. Amos was not thrilled with his assignment, having heard about Micah and Nathan.
ELI: You're my last hope, Amos. This is the toughest assignment I've ever given you. But you are faithful and wise. Perhaps you can talk sense to those farmers.
AMOS: You've been good to me and my family, sir. After all you've done for me, this is the least I can do for you. I will do my best.
NARRATOR: Later, Amos arrived at the farm.
ACHAN: What kind of fool is Eli? Does he think that you can do what those other two could not? If he sends one hundred men, our answer is the same!
NARRATOR: Before Amos could even open his mouth, the farmers jumped on him and beat him. Not even Amos was able to reason with those wicked men!
  When Eli heard about Amos, he was again deeply distressed.
ELI: I have sent three of my best men to the land of Erets and they have mistreated each of them. There is only one person I can send now, and that is my son, Jeshua. They will respect him as they would me. Surely, they will listen to him!
NARRATOR: So Eli called his son, Jeshua, and explained to him his mission.
JESHUA: If it is your will, father, I will go.
ELI: Just tell them you are my son. They will respect you.
NARRATOR: So Jeshua and his crew departed. Days later, the farmers spotted a stranger coming down from the hills.
ACHAN: Could it be that Eli is stupid enough to send another messenger?
NARRATOR: As Jeshua neared, their talk and wonder increased.
ACHAN: Who is this one? I don't recognize him. Is he one of Eli's men?
NARRATOR: Jeshua stood before Achan and his men. They looked him over carefully, before any words were said.
ACHAN: Who are you, stranger, and what can we do for you?

JESHUA: I have come to collect my father's share of the harvest.
ACHAN: You are Eli's son?
JESHUA: I am.
ACHAN: Why would Eli send his son here after we have beat up three of his best men? He must be dumber than I thought.
JESHUA: My father is fair and just. He has sent me, hoping that you will listen to his son and honor his demand for his share.
NARRATOR: An evil and ugly grin appeared on Achan's face. As he looked at the other farmers, they began to grin also. Then, the grins broke into wild laughs.
ACHAN: His son! The one who will someday receive the land! Now is our chance, boys! The land is ours!
NARRATOR: Achan motioned the laughing to stop. He walked up to Jeshua. Everyone was quiet.
ACHAN: Yes, we will treat you differently, son of Eli. The others we merely beat up, but you we will kill! Then we will be the inheritors of the land! How does that sound?
NARRATOR: But Jeshua did not answer. Even as Achan signaled to his men to perform the execution, Jeshua remained silent.

When Eli heard the news of his son's death, he did not have to think. He quicky gathered a small army of soldiers and set off for the land of Erets. They arrived at night while the farmers were sleeping. Eli knocked on the door of his house. Achan answered, wiping the sleep from his eyes.
ACHAN: Sir! This is indeed a surprise. Please come in.
ELI: I have not come to visit, you unfaithful servant!
ACHAN: Unfaithful? But sir, look at the bountiful harvest. We have worked hard all season on your land.
ELI: Yes, in order to keep the fruit of the harvest for yourselves! I sent three messengers to you, and you beat each one. Yet I still had compassion for you. So I sent my only son, my heir, and you brutally killed him! You did this hoping to receive the land yourself. You are wicked people! I have been fair and good to you, but you have rejected my goodness. Now you will reap your reward!
NARRATOR: The band of soldiers began to light their torches.
ACHAN: No, master, please! We are sorry! Here, we give you your share! Please forgive us!
ELI: Mercy has run out for you! This land will belong to the poor people in the land of Erets. The proud will have it no more! The poor will be thankful to have it, and they will not try to steal it from me.

Story Application

"Does this story remind you of something God our Heavenly Father did for us? Let's rename the characteristics in the story to explain how God did this. Eli was God the Father. Who did Micah, Nathan and Amos represent? (The prophets of the Old Testament.) Who did the farmers stand for? (Evil people here on earth.) What is the land of Erets? (The world.) Who did Jeshua stand for? (God the Son.) Who did the poor people represent? (Those who would obey God and live to serve Him.)

"According to the story, why did God have to send His Son? (Because the people did not listen to the prophets.) We need to keep in mind that although the story ends with Jeshua dead, in real life God the Son did not remain dead after He was crucified for our sins, but He rose after three days.

"God the Father has sent God the Son into a sinful world in order to save it (John 3:17). But people even today are still rejecting the Son. What do you think God will do to those who reject His Son? (Punish them with death.) What about those who accept His Son? (Make them heirs of all his riches.)

"See how important God the Son is? And see how important is it for us to accept Him? (Use this opportunity to introduce Jesus to anyone who has not accepted Him already. Be sensitive. See chapter two for guidelines, if needed.) We should always be thankful to God the Father for loving us enough to send His Son. Let's thank Him in prayer right now."

The Parable Frieze

A frieze is a series of pictures on a long strip of paper that tells a continuous story. Draw a frieze about "The Landowner's Son" on butcher paper, shelf paper or roll ends which you can probably purchase from your local newspaper.

Assign different parts of the story to each member of the family and illustrate the entire parable in full color using felt pens.

Scrambled Words

Divide the family into two teams (a younger person and an older person on each team). Give both groups two scrambled verses to unscramble. The words of each verse should be written on separate small pieces of paper so that they can be rearranged at will. Use Matthew 11:28 and John 3:36.

Once both teams have correctly unscrambled the two verses, discuss their meaning. Both verses deal with the importance of coming to Jesus.

Crossword Puzzle

In the "Bible Activity Section is a crossword puzzle that gives many names and titles of God's Son. Fill out the puzzle with your children, giving them an opportunity to fill in the blanks, if they can, before they look up the verses. A good follow-up on this activity is to discuss each of the names and what they mean.

FAMILY FUN ACTIVITIES

Modeling Clay

Go to an arts and crafts store and purchase modeling clay for use by your family during this fun period. Let them make whatever they want.

Finger Painting

You will probably only have time to do one of these two activity suggestions. If you choose to do finger painting, buy some finger paints from your local arts and crafts store. It is possible to make the paint yourself, but it would be wise to check in an arts and crafts book (available in most public libraries) for exact instructions. Again, let your children make what they want, using the following procedure:

1. Moisten a sheet of highly glazed paper on both sides by drawing it through a shallow pan of clear water.
2. Spread the paper smoothly on a flat surface.
3. Cover the surface with paint, using the palm and fingers to spread it around. Apply different colors as desired.
4. Using your fingers, fist, forearm, sponge, etc. make your design or picture. If you don't like it—erase it and start over.
5. Let your paintings dry on a smooth surface; press on the back with a hot iron to smooth out the wrinkles.

Chapter Eleven
God the Holy Spirit

YOUR PERSONAL PREPARATION

Introduction

With the increased focus on the ministry of the Holy Spirit in recent years, it is amazing that many Christians are not certain what the Bible teaches about Him.

It is basic to our knowledge of this very important member of the Godhead to realize that without the Holy Spirit there would be no gospel, no faith, no Church and no Christianity. He is responsible for all we enjoy as Christians today. He is God actively involved in our lives.

There is much that can be studied about the Holy Spirit: His nature, His purpose, His activity. But perhaps the best way to introduce Him to children is by exploring what He does. This lesson centers on the ministries of the Holy Spirit. Be careful to point out to your family that the Holy Spirit is a person, He is God, and He has many ministries.

Basic Bible Teaching

1. The Holy Spirit is a Person.
   a. He dwells with us. John 14:17.
   b. He teaches and brings remembrances. John 14:26.
   c. He bears witness of Jesus. John 15:26.
   d. He convicts of sin. John 16:8.
   e. He sends out workers. Acts 13:4.
   f. He forbids actions. Acts 16:6, 7.
   g. He can be lied to and tempted. Acts 5:1-9.
   h. He can be resisted. Acts 7:51.
   i. He can be grieved. Ephesians 4:30.
2. The Holy Spirit is God.
   a. He can be blasphemed against. Matthew 12:31.
   b. He is equated with the Father and Son. Matthew 28:19; 2 Corinthians 13:14.
   c. He is called God. Acts 5:3, 4; 2 Corinthians 3:17, 18.

3. The Holy Spirit has many ministries.
   a. He gives gifts to the Church. 1 Corinthians 12-14.
   b. He gives spiritual fruit. Galatians 5:22, 23.
   c. He fills us. Ephesians 5:18.
   d. He comforts. John 14:16, 17.
   e. He seals. Ephesians 1:13; 4:30.
   f. He indwells. Romans 8:11.
   g. He assures of salvation. Romans 8:16.

Lesson Objectives

1. That your family will understand that the Holy Spirit is God.

2. That your family will understand that the Holy Spirit wants to fill and empower them to shine for Christ.

3. That the family will want to be controlled by the Holy Spirit.

Things You'll Need

1. For "Bible Notetaking," paper and pencils.

2. For "Flashlight Object Lesson," a flashlight with batteries, a small dirty rag with these words written on it: "Our Good Works—Isaiah 64:6."

3. For "Bible Drawing Time," crayons, felt pens or water colors, and paper.

4. For "The Envelope of God's Love," a small picture of each member of the family and an envelope addressed to God.

5. For "The Blue Book," several copies of Campus Crusade for Christ's small booklet, "Have You Made the Wonderful Discovery of the Spirit-Filled Life," on the ministry of the Holy Spirit. These are available in bookstores or may be ordered through Campus Crusade for Christ, Arrowhead Springs, Calif. 92414.

6. For the "Family Fun Activity," several of your household's most popular Christian albums.

THE LESSON

Bible Notetaking

Read Acts 2, in The Living Bible, about the introduction of the Holy Spirit to the world and the birth of the Church. Before you begin reading, make certain each family member has a pencil and a piece of paper. Instruct everyone to take "notes" on what you are going to read. The notes can be written or drawn depending on the child's age.

After you have finished reading, give a few extra minutes so that everyone can finish their notes. Then have each person explain what he has written or drawn, and why. (The notes should go into their notebooks.)

Flashlight Object Lesson

"God the Holy Spirit wants to give each of us something that is very important. What am I holding? (A flashlight.) This flashlight is like you and me. What is a flashlight made for? (Yes, to give off light.)

"And the Bible tells us, 'You are the light of the world . . . Let your light shine before men in such a way that they may see your good works, and glorify your Father who is in heaven' (Matthew 5:14a, 16, NASB).

"Okay, let's turn this flashlight on. Mmm. It doesn't seem to be shining too brightly, does it? Let's open it up and see if we can find the problem.

"Well look at this, there's a small dirty rag in it. (Pull out the rag, but don't reveal the fact that there are no batteries in the flashlight.) Look what's written on the rag. (Let the kids read 'Our Good Works—Isaiah 64:6,' which should be written on the rag.)

"Who will look up and read Isaiah 64:6? Thank you. It tells us that all our 'good works' are the same as filthy rags. Now that we have taken away the good works done in our own power, let's see how the flashlight works. (Close it and turn it on.)

"Mmm. Still no light. Let's look in it again. Well, look in there—no batteries. We don't have any power. You and I can't shine our lights either unless we have some power. Here, let's put in these two batteries which represent the Holy Spirit, because God's Word says we are to be filled or empowered with the Holy Spirit (Ephesians 5:18).

"Well, the light is finally shining. That's one of the things that the Holy Spirit does for us. He gives us the power to shine for God. He fills us up with Himself."

Bible Drawing Time

Using crayons, felt markers or water colors, have each member of the family draw two pictures of themselves. One will show them without the Holy Spirit's control and power, the other with His control. Make certain the two drawings are labeled and placed in their notebooks.

The Envelope of God's Love

"We each have a picture of ourselves. Let's drop them into this envelope (do not seal it). Who is the envelope addressed to? (God.)

"Did you know that as a believer in the Lord Jesus Christ, you belong to Him? Who is the only Person who can open this envelope? (God.) Why? (Because it is addressed to Him.) But look, I am opening the envelope and taking a picture out! Now who says God is the only one who can open the envelope?

"Was it right for me to take a person out of God's envelope? (No.) Who do you think would ever want to steal us away from God? (Satan.) What could be done to this envelope to keep someone from reaching in and taking a picture out? (Seal the envelope.)

"Okay, I'll put the picture back in and lick the flap. Look (shake the envelope). The pictures can't fall out and no one can reach in and take any out. To get the pictures out, the seal must be broken, and only God, the receiver, is allowed to do that.

"When we accept Jesus as our personal Lord and Savior, we belong to Him. But we do not live with Him in heaven right away; we are waiting for the day that He will come and receive us. It is as though we have been placed in an envelope addressed to God. Then, God the Holy Spirit comes along and seals the envelope with us safe inside.

"In the meantime, Satan cannot touch the contents of that envelope! Therefore, when we accept the Lord Jesus, we need never worry about losing Him or being taken away from Him, because God the Holy Spirit has sealed us!"

Bible Drill

"There are many Bible verses which tell us about the Holy Spirit. I'm going to call out a Bible reference. Let's see who can find it first. After everyone has found it, I'll call on someone to read the verse and tell us about the Holy Spirit according to that verse."

1. Verses which show that the Holy Spirit is a Person:
—1 Corinthians 2:11. (He has an intellect.)
—Romans 8:27 or 15:30. (He has emotions.)
—1 Corinthians 12:11. (He has a will.)
2. Verses which show that the Holy Spirit is God:
—Acts 5:3, 4:2 Corinthians 3:17, 18.

3. Verses which show what the Holy Spirit does for us:
—John 14:16, 17. (Comforts us.)
—Ephesians 1:13; 4:30. (Seals us.)
—John 16:7-9. (Convicts us of sin.)
—Romans 8:16. (Assures us of salvation.)
—Ephesians 5:18. (Fills us.)

Memory Time

Have the family work on memorizing Ephesians 5:18. Discuss what it means to be drunk (and controlled) by wine and what it means to be controlled and filled by the Holy Spirit.

The Blue Book

For older family members, obtain copies of Campus Crusade for Christ's small booklet on the filling of the Holy Spirit, "Have You Made the Wonderful Discovery of the Spirit-Filled Life." Discuss each point made in the book.

Prayer and Discussion Time

1. Ask the family what they've learned about the person and ministry of the Holy Spirit.
2. Ask them how they would know if they were controlled by the Holy Spirit. (Good evidence would be the fruit of the Spirit.)
3. Ask if they want to be filled right now. (If yes, give an opportunity to pray, in faith believing, for His filling right now.)
4. Have a closing prayer time.

FAMILY FUN ACTIVITY

Top Tunes

Have the family members pull out their favorite Christian albums and select their favorite songs. Have a "Top Tune" time, allowing each person to play his favorite song while the others listen attentively. If you have a small family, you might want to give each person two or even three selections. Make certain everyone listens quietly to each selection as it is played—this can be a good time of worship.

Chapter Twelve
The Three-In-Oneness-Of-God

YOUR PERSONAL PREPARATION

Introduction

Sometimes we tend to compartmentalize God and to limit Him. We like to think (from a doctrinal point of view) that we have Him all figured out. But God is more complex than any conception our finite minds can imagine. If we could totally understand Him, He would not be God.

One of the most challenging truths of the Christian faith is the notoriously difficult doctrine of the "three-in-oneness" of God, or the Trinity. No matter how hard we try to comprehend and explain it, the doctrine will always be a little beyond the limited capacities of our human minds.

Throughout Scripture we are plainly taught that although God is plural in personality (Genesis 1:26), He is also one God (1 Timothy 2:5).

This concept of God's three-in-oneness will be simplistically illustrated to children during this lesson. But no illustration about the Trinity is completely adequate—and the ones used in this lesson will be no different. Use them realizing they will never fully explain this difficult doctrine.

Fortunately, most children will accept you explanation of God's three-in-oneness as completely logical. Jesus made it plain that we adults need to come to the Kingdom of God with the faith of a child. Perhaps we need to exhibit that same childlike faith when it comes to doctrines like the Trinity.

Basic Bible Teaching

1. God is One in essence. Deuteronomy 6:4.
2. God is One in purpose. Matthew 28:19.
3. God is plural in personhood. Genesis 1:26, 27; Matthew 28:19.
4. The Father is God. Ephesians 4:6.
5. The Son is God. 2 Peter 1:1.
6. The Holy Spirit is God. Acts 5:3, 4.

Lesson Objectives

1. That your family will understand more clearly the three-in-oneness of God.
2. That the family will understand that we do not worship three gods, but a Triune God.
3. That the family will know that our God is indeed God.

Things You'll Need

1. For "Is Light White?" you'll need a prism, a piece of cardboard (or hot plate), a small pan, and three ice cubes.
2. For the "Three-in-Oneness Object Lesson" you'll need a stove burner (or hot plate), a small pan, and three ice cubes.
3. For "Match Riddles," you will need a box of wood matches (or Q-tips).

THE LESSON

The Mysterious Dots

In the Bible Activity Section is a square entitled: "The Mysterious Dots." Cut the square out, making certain you do not leave any of the square on the paper, and show it to the children in your family.

"There are four dots on this square. They can be tied together with two straight lines. Can any of you figure out how to do it?"

Probably no one will be able to figure out how it can be done with only two lines. They will suggest making the lines curve and other possibilities which don't really deal with the problem.

Explain that this puzzle is similar to God's three-in-oneness. Because we cannot completely understand the Trinity, does not make it any less true.

"The Old Testament presents a problem just like those dots. The Scriptures tell us that God is one God, yet it often refers to Him as more than one Person. How can that be explained?

"To understand what the Old Testament is teaching about God, we must have a larger frame of reference. The New Testament gives that to us. It presents the fact of the three-in-oneness of God more clearly, so that we can begin to understand it.

"Take a look at those dots again. The reason you could not connect them with two straight lines was because you restricted yourself to the paper. (Draw two lines which go off the paper and would therefore join.)

"That's why we were given the whole Bible: so that we could understand about Him more fully. But even then, the Bible doesn't tell us everything about God. Some day we will meet Him face to face—and then we'll understand everything."

A Look in The Book

Have your family look at some of these Old Testament verses and talk about them.

Genesis 1:26

Genesis 3:22

Genesis 11:6, 7

Isaiah 6:8

Is Light White?

For this demonstration you will need a prism which you can purchase in a hobby store or one which specializes in scientific or photographic equipment. It is best to do this experiment before it gets dark outside, so that you can use light from the sun.

Put a small hole in a large piece of cardboard or tagboard. Place the cardboard over a sunlit window so that only one small beam enters the room through the opening.

At this point you will want to discuss the nature of light and ask what color it is. A good book from the library will arm you with more interesting facts.

Place the prism in the thin shaft of light that the cardboard is allowing through the window. On top of a piece of white paper, turn the prism until the "white light" separates to reveal its many colors of the rainbow.

Discuss the fact that light looks "white," but in reality is composed of all the colors of the rainbow. In the same way God is one God with three distinct personalities.

The Oneness of God

"We do not believe in three Gods, we believe in a Triune God. This was very important when the Bible was written. People believed in all kinds of gods, each of whom had one job. Can you think of any of those gods you've heard about in school or church?" (You may have to help here. Suggest the sun god, the rain god, the goddess of love, the god of darkness, the god of fertility, the god of war, the god of the hills, etc.)

"Long ago God revealed He is One to the Israelites. Their God was different from the so-called gods of all the peoples who lived nearby. The Jews had one God—all the others had many. (Read Deuteronomy 6:4 and discuss why this verse is so important.)

"Our God is one God. In His Book, the Bible, He tells us that He is the God who made everything. (Read the story of Paul's sermon in Athens; Acts 17:22-31 from The Living Bible.)

Three-in-Oneness Object Lesson

"How can God be One—and yet three? Of course it is a mystery. But we can do a simple experiment that will help us understand God a little more clearly."

In the kitchen, place three ice cubes in a flat pan on a burner on top of the stove. Turn the burner as high as it will go to speed up the experiment.

"What is an ice cube made of? (Water.) All this ice cube is, is frozen water.

"What is happening to the cubes? (They're beginning to melt.) So we now have water in two forms: solid and liquid.

"But wait! Look very closely—do you see the water taking still another form? (Yes, steam or a gas.)

"Now look at the whole picture. In this pan we have water in three forms at one time. What are they? (Solid, liquid and gas.) We have three substances here, yet it is still all one thing: water.

"Remember the last three lessons? We talked about three Persons. Who are they? (Father, Son and Holy Spirit.) Did you know that these three Persons are all God? Not three gods, but one God in three Persons. Just like the water which we saw was three-in-one, we have a God who is three-in-One.

"This idea of God is hard to understand, but God knows who He is, and He tells us in His Word that He is three-in-One. Another word for 'three-in-One' is 'Trinity.' So, our God is a Trinity.

"Let's read a portion of God's Word that mentions the Trinity: Father, Son and Holy Spirit. (Read together Ephesians 4:4-6 from The Living Bible, taking each of the three verses one at a time. After each verse, ask which Person of the Trinity it is talking about.)

Bible Study

Look up the following Bible references which contain each of the three members of the Trinity. See if the family can spot which inference applies to which member of the Godhead.

1. Matthew 28:19. (The Great Commission.)
2. 2 Corinthians 13:14. (In a benediction.)
3. 1 Peter 1:2. (The ministry of the Three.)
4. Matthew 3:16, 17. (The baptism of Christ.)
5. John 14:16, 17. (Christ prays for the Comforter.)

Trinity Illustration

In the Bible Activity Section there is a Trinity illustration. Have your children look at this wheel and discuss the truths it contains. You may want them to copy it so that each child can place the illustration in his notebook.

FAMILY FUN ACTIVITIES

Match Riddles

1. Make three squares by the use of ten matches as shown below. Tell your family that they are to remove only two matches and leave two complete squares. (The trick is accomplished by removing the matches labeled "x" and "y".)

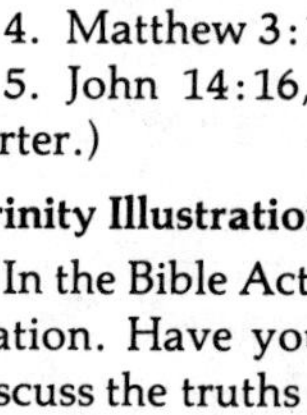

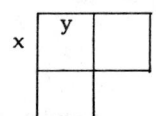

2. Arrange twelve matches in four squares as shown below. Tell your family that they are to rearrange three matches to come up with three squares instead of four. (The trick is accomplished by removing the two matches from the upper lefthand corner and the match in the lower right-hand corner. Use these three matches to form a new square at the lower right.)

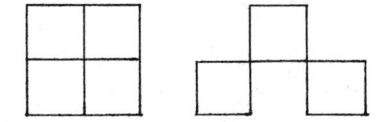

3. Use twenty-four matches arranged in nine squares as shown below. Tell your family to remove six matches so that only three complete squares are left. (The trick is accomplished by removing the six matches marked "x". This will leave two squares inside the big square.)

V. What Is God Like?

Chapter Thirteen

God Is Holy

YOUR PERSONAL PREPARATION

Introduction

Holiness is a difficult doctrine for us to understand, because we know no one who is holy. Holiness is entirely foreign to us, except as we see glimpses of God Himself in the Bible. We can only stand in wonder and awe at such a perfect and righteous God who has somehow been able to redeem sinful man by way of the cross.

This is the first lesson that looks at God's attributes. When you ask your family, "What is the most important character quality that God possesses?", most will answer "love." But holiness is God's first and foremost moral characteristic.

In everything God does, He is holy. It is the essence of His moral nature. He can never temporarily lay aside this holiness as He can with other attributes.

A holy God cannot stand sin—it is against His nature. Therefore, when God judges sin, He is still holy, even though He is not necessarily loving. On the other hand, when the Father shows love and mercy, He is not exercising His attribute of justice—but again He is still holy. In everything He does, we can see God's holy nature shining through.

As you present this lesson, you will want to stress both what God is like and the fact that His Word says, "Be holy, as I am holy." The more we know about God, the more we will be able to let God's Spirit fill us with His divine character qualities.

Basic Bible Teaching

1. God is holy by nature. Leviticus 19:2; 21:8; Psalm 111:9.
2. God's name is holy. Leviticus 22:2; Psalm 106:47.
3. God deserves our exclusive service because He is holy. Joshua 24:19-24.
4. God's holiness sets Him apart from all others. 1 Samuel 2:2.
5. God's holiness causes praise. Psalm 103:1; Isaiah 6:3.
6. God is therefore a righteous God. Isaiah 5:16.
7. God's temple is holy. 1 Corinthians 3:17.

Lesson Objectives

1. That the family will come to realize that God is holy, perfect and pure.
2. That the family will desire to be like God in His holiness.
3. That the family will ask God to be holy through them.

Things You'll Need

1. For "Decode the Verses," you should have a mirror and a dictionary handy.
2. For "Think Tank," you will need notebook paper and pencils for everyone.
3. For "Create a Psalm," the younger children will

need magazines with pictures in them to help them illustrate the family Psalm.

4. For the "Family Fun Activities," you will need various sports equipment depending on which activities you choose to do.

THE LESSON
A Look in the Book

"What is the most important character quality that God possesses?" (Let the family members discuss their answer to this question. You might suggest such qualities as justice, love, truth, holiness, etc. to give them food for thought. The answer, of course, is holiness, but don't answer this question yet.)

"Much of the Old Testament was written by men of God called 'prophets.' Do you know what a prophet is?" (He is a man whom God chose to speak through when He wanted to tell the people something. The prophet spoke the words of God.)

"One of the most important prophets in the Bible is Isaiah. Can you guess what book he wrote?" (Right, he wrote the book of Isaiah.)

"We're going to read about the time God allowed the prophet Isaiah to see a magnificent sight. This experience is found in Isaiah 6:1-7." (Use The Living Bible to read this passage to the family.)

"Who was it Isaiah saw? (The Lord.)

"Try to imagine what this vision which Isaiah saw must have been like. The Lord was sitting on a high throne in His temple. All around Him were flying seraphs. Do you know what a seraph is? (An angel).

"Each of these seraphs had six wings. They used two to cover their faces, two to cover their feet, and two to fly with! The answer is in the passage. (God is holy—but again, don't answer it yet.)

"The seraphs were all singing a loud and beautiful song. What were they singing about? (The Lord.) The singing was so loud it shook the temple. Can you imagine singing that loud in Church? Notice too, that the sanctuary was filled with smoke.

"The song called Him something three times. It said, 'Love, love, love,' didn't it? No, it said 'Holy, holy, holy.' When Isaiah saw the Lord, he compared himself to Him and was terrified! What did he say about himself? (See verse five.) He said this because God is holy. What does it mean to be holy? (Clean, pure, good, righteous—without sin or guilt of any kind.)

"God is holy. That's why Isaiah felt so unclean. Because God is holy those who are impure or imperfect cannot come into His direct presence.

"Do you know what God's most important character quality is now? (That's right, it's holiness.) The Bible tells us a little about what God's face is like. (Read Revelation 1:16 from The Living Bible.) It says His face is like the power of the sun—too bright to look at!

"What about those angels? Why did they have to cover themselves before God? (Because He is holy and they are not.)

"What about us? What are we like compared to God? (Yes, we're sinful.) God never sins, because He is holy. It was a frightening experience for Isaiah to look at God, because he knew he was a sinner.

"About 700 years before Isaiah's experience, Moses also saw the Lord. (Read Exodus 3:1-6 in The Living Bible.) The Lord appeared to him in a burning bush. The Bible says that Moses covered his face with his hands, for he was afraid to look at God (v. 6). Why was he afraid? (Because he was a sinner and God is holy.)

"Later Moses actually asked to see God's glory. Let's read Exodus 33:18-23 in The Living Bible and see what happened.

"Did Moses actually see God's face? (No.) Why not? (Men may not see God and live, because His glory is too great.)

"Just think, the Bible tells us that someday we will see God face-to-face (1 John 3:2). But we don't have to be afraid, because we will be holy just like He is then.

"What do you think it's like to be holy? How can we begin to be holy today?"

Decode the Verses

In the Bible Activity Section there are two verses which need to be decoded. Have the members of the family study the verse until they can read them. (All the words are spelled backwards and can be read with a mirror.)

Once they can read the verses correctly (1 Peter 1:15, 16) discuss their meaning. Ask someone to look up the words "holy" and "holiness" in the dictionary so that all will know what God wants us to do.

Think Tank

Have the family members enter the "think tank." In the tank, they will try to think of ways they can be holy like God. On a piece of paper have each person list ways he can show holiness. The children will place their sheets in their notebooks after they are finished.

Memory Time

Work on memorizing 1 Peter 1:16. For teenagers, have them work on verse 15 too. After the family has looked at the passage for a few minutes, have everyone close their Bibles.

One child will say the first word of 1 Peter 1:16. The next person says the next word. Continue until someone misses. That person can look up the verse and say the correct word. See how many tries it takes before no one has to look up the verse.

Create a Psalm

Read Psalm 99 as a group and discuss how David praised God for His holiness.

Have the family write their own Psalm of praise about God. Encourage each member to add something. Concentrate on praising God for what He has done and for His perfect character qualities. Take care to praise Him for His holiness.

Younger children should illustrate the family's Psalm with pictures cut out of magazines.

FAMILY FUN ACTIVITIES

For your fun activities, play any of the following outdoor games. You may only have time to play one of them.

Play Catch

This activity doesn't take much equipment and is usually something that all children enjoy. If your youngsters have baseball or softball gloves, so much the better.

Play Four-Squares

Using a large rubber ball, play a popular elementary school game: four-square. With a piece of chalk, draw four large squares on the driveway. The squares are numbered one through four. The person in square number one is the server.

The object of this game is to become the server and stay there. The ball is bounced, then hit with the flat of the hand into another square. If a player holds the ball, hits it on the line, or it hits his body, he is "out" and loses his place. If he is the server, he must go to the end of the line (of those waiting to come in) or back to the number four position. Everyone else moves up and number two is now the server.

Play Tennis or Racketball

If you have the equipment, tennis is a fun family game. As it takes younger children a while to become proficient at this game, you will have to exercise your patience if they are beginners.

Another popular sport that is growing tremendously in popularity is racketball. The game is played on a handball court (usually fully enclosed) and requires much less initial ability than does tennis. If there are courts in your area (either public or school ones), this is a good game to look into.

Chapter Fourteen

God Is Just

YOUR PERSONAL PREPARATION

Introduction

One of the characteristics of God that is presented most often in Scripture is God's justice; but somehow, it is difficult for most of us to accept or truly appreciate what the justice of God means.

When we think of justice, what we so often think of is punishment for sin. None of us likes to think that our God is a God of judgment—a God who sends sinners to hell. We must understand this attribute of God fully, or we will struggle with God's justice—feeling He is partial, unfair and too severe in His punishment.

God's basic moral nature is absolutely holy. As such He cannot stand the sight of sin. He has said, "The soul that sins, it shall surely die." God does not hate the sinner, but He does hate sin. And His unchanging nature has committed Himself to a course of action: all sin must be punished.

But fortunately there is more to God's nature than holiness and justice. God is also a God of mercy and love. Because sin must be paid for, He has provided a substitute justice for all those who will respond to it.

Jesus died on the cross for the sins of the entire world. Because He is God, His sacrifice is capable of satisfying the penalty for sin.

But Christ's death is meaningless to all those who do not accept what He has done. Like the man who refuses a pardon from the President of the United States—so is the man or woman who does not accept Jesus and what He did on the cross.

As you teach this lesson you will want to stress the fact that God is perfectly just—which means He is perfectly fair. It may be hard for us to see this fairness from our limited perspective, but we can be sure our holy God knows exactly what He's doing in every situation.

Basic Bible Teaching

1. God is just. Deuteronomy 32:4.
2. God is a righteous judge. 2 Timothy 4:8.
3. God loves justice. Psalm 33:5; 37:28.
4. God's throne is founded on justice and righteousness. Psalm 89:14; 97:2.
5. God's judgement is just. Psalm 9:8; 96:10, 13; Revelation 16:7.
6. God has fixed a day when He will judge the world. Acts 17:31.
7. Jesus Christ will rule in justice. Isaiah 9:7; Acts 17:31.
8. Jesus came into the world for justice. John 9:39; 5:22, 27; 3:19.
9. Jesus came to put away sin once and for all by the sacrifice of Himself. Hebrews 9:26; 9:14.
10. All men must die (physically) because of sin, but those who respond to Christ will have eternal life. Hebrews 9:27, 28; 2:9, 14, 15; Romans 6:23.

Lesson Objectives

1. That the family will understand that God is just.
2. That the family will know that God is always fair and therefore worthy of our trust.

Things You'll Need

1. For "Sin in the Garden," have colored pencils and paper for your younger children to draw the story. This can be done while you present the material in "Dealing with a Problem."
2. For the "Family Fun Activities" you will want to provide several newspapers and plain paper for paper airplanes.

THE LESSON

Sin in the Garden

Read the story of the Fall in Genesis 2 and 3, from *The Living Bible*, concentrating on God's judgment on sin. Point out Genesis 2:17 and how Adam deliberately disobeyed that commandment.

Have each member of the family choose a character and act out the story. The different parts include Adam, Eve, the Serpent and God.

Discussion Time

Once you have acted out the story of the Fall, discuss its meaning. Have the younger children draw the garden story while you discuss it with older family members—or they may do it when you present the material on "Dealing with a Problem." The following discussion questions will help you begin.

1. "Why did God say that Adam and Eve were not to eat of the tree of the knowledge of good and evil?"
2. "Why did the Serpent (Satan) try to make Adam and his wife disobey God?"
3. "Why did they disobey God?"
4. "What punishment did Adam and Eve receive?"
5. "Could God have forgiven and forgotten about the punishment and still been fair?"

Story Time

"A famous traveling evangelist was driving his car down a back road in a rural area when he suddenly realized he was being followed by a police car.

" 'Do you know what the speed limit on this road is?' the officer asked when the evangelist had pulled over.

" 'No, I'm afraid I don't,' replied the Christian.

" 'Well, it's 30 m.p.h. and you were doing 45! I'm going to write you up. You'll have to take this ticket into the next town. The judge is a barber, so you'll have to go to the barbershop to pay the fine.'

"So the offender drove into town and pulled up to the local barbershop. He entered the building and showed the ticket to the man who was cutting hair.

" 'Court will be in session as soon as I finish cutting this man's hair. Have a seat.'

"In a few moments, the haircut was completed and the barber sat behind a desk. Picking up his gavel, he banged it on the desk.

" 'Court is in session. I see by this ticket you were driving 45 m.p.h. in a 30 m.p.h. zone on Highway 9. How do you plead?'

" 'Guilty as charged, your Honor.'

" 'I fine you fifteen dollars.'

"The evangelist pulled his wallet out of his back pocket, when the judge suddenly asked another question.

" 'Don't I know you? Aren't you the minister who is on television?'

" 'I hate to admit it, after getting this ticket, but I am.'

" 'Well, put it there,' the judge said, holding out his hand. 'You've had a tremendous influence on my life. My family and I have really enjoyed watching your TV program.'

"They continued to talk together and the minister put his wallet back into his pocket. He was about to leave when the judge said: 'That will still be fifteen dollars.'

"Once again the evangelist reached for his wallet.

" 'Wait a minute,' the judge said. 'I can't let you pay that ticket. I'm going to pay it for you.'

" 'So the judge pulled out his own wallet and clipped fifteen dollars to the ticket and put it into his desk. Justice had been paid in full—by the judge.

"Isn't that like what God does for us? Somebody had to pay the penalty for our sin—so He sent His Son to do it for us."

Dealing with a Problem

Over the years many people have asked how a loving God could possibly send people to hell. They claim that they could never respond to a God who could be so cold and unfair.

If this logic has effected your older teenagers (or they will soon be exposed to it,) use this section to discuss this so-called problem.

First, state the problem question: "How can a loving God send men to hell?" Then, point by point, take your family through each of the following discussion questions:

1. "What is God's standard?" (Holiness.)
2. "Would God be God if He announced the penalty for sin and then did not enforce it?" (No, he would be a liar.)
3. "Does God want to send men to hell?" (No. 2 Timothy 2:4; 2 Peter 3:9.)
4. "Who really determines who goes to hell?" (The man or woman who rejects God's pardon through Christ. John 3:17, 18.)
5. "What are the wages for sin?" (Death, according to Romans 6:23.)
6. "God *is* a God of love. But He is also a God of what? (Holiness and justice.) It is God's holiness, justice and fairness that demands that sin be paid for. If we don't accept Jesus' payment, we will have to pay for it ourselves."

How Just Are We?

"When we look at the justice of God we realize that it is perfect. God knows everything there is about a man when He exercises judgment. We are told that He will judge the very secrets of men (Romans 2:16). He is completely impartial (Romans 2:11), and will judge every man according to his deeds (Romans 2:6).

"What about us? Are we just in our judgments? No human judge or referee or umpire is perfect—and as such they will make mistakes. They judge as they see fit—based upon the knowledge they have and the rules or standards which they have been given.

"Christians have a perfect standard by which to judge the actions of the world around them. That standard is the Word of God. But we must always be wary of passing judgment on others when we don't live up to the standard ourselves. (Romans 2:1-3). In fact, we will be judged by our own judgment (Matthew 7:1, 2).

"God tells us that judgment belongs to Him (Hebrews 10:30). He is the One who will take care of evil. Our job here on earth is to exercise forgiveness over and over (Matthew 18:21, 22). We are to trust ourselves to that faithful Judge. We are never to take our own revenge but leave room for the wrath of God (Romans 12:17-21.)

"Let's read the parable of the unforgiving servant in Matthew 18:23-35. It has a lot to say about the importance of forgiveness which leaves room for the justice of God."

FAMILY FUN ACTIVITIES

Fun with Paper

1. Make a "Paper Tree." To make a paper tree, have your children take two double pages out of the comic section of a newspaper. Cut the newspaper the long way. This gives four pieces half the width of the paper and two widths long.

Have your children roll up one piece so that the center is about two fingers wide. Roll it the short way. When there is approximately one fourth of the paper left, place the second page inside the first and continue rolling so that the second sheet covers the first. Insert all pages in the same way until everything is rolled together. Tape the complete roll in the center so that it will not come apart.

Now have your children cut down about halfway from one end with a pair of scissors. Make a second cut opposite the first. Then cut the two parts down the middle in the same way. Have your children take hold of the center piece on the cut end and pull up.

2. Make "paper airplanes." Try your hand at making several different kinds of paper airplanes. If you had little experience with them when you were a child, your children will probably be able to give you some help. After your family has created several different "models," go outside and see who can throw theirs the farthest, the highest, and keep it up the longest.

Chapter Fifteen
God Is Love

YOUR PERSONAL PREPARATION

Introduction

The Bible tells us that "God is love" (1 John 4:16). That statement is not an all-inclusive definition of God, as there are times when He does not show love (i.e. when He sends a sinner to hell), but God is the summation of all true love. God is total love. Take Him out of the world and there would be no love or righteousness left.

The purpose of this lesson is to help the family understand that God loves each of us completely and He wants us to learn to love like He loves.

What we think is love is often veiled selfishness. Many times we do things for others because we want to receive a reward for our actions.

God's love was offered before we asked for it (Romans 5:8; 1 John 4:19), it can never be taken away (Romans 8:35-39) and it is not based upon what we did to deserve it.

We will never have a clear picture of what true godly love is until we understand what God is like. Use this week's lesson to focus both on how God loves and how He wants us to love.

Basic Bible Teaching

1. God is love. 1 John 4:8, 16.
2. God's love is too big for us to fully comprehend. Ephesians 3:17-19.
3. God's love can be experienced. 1 John 4:7, 8, 16-19.
4. God's love is shown in His Son. John 3:16; 1 John 3:16; 4:9, 10.
5. God's love is sure. Romans 8:35-39.
6. The Father loves those who love the Son. John 16:27; 14:21.

Lesson Objectives

1. That the family will understand that God loves us because it is His nature—we've done nothing to deserve it.
2. That the family will understand that true godly love is completely unselfish.
3. That the family will begin to love like God loves.

Things You'll Need

1. For the "Quickie Quiz," you will need paper and pencils for each in your family.
2. In "Cartoon Time," have paper and paste ready to glue in new words for the drawings in the Bible Activity Section.
3. For "What Is Love?" and "Let's Compare" you will need paper and pencils.
4. For the "Toothpaste Race," each member of the family will need their personal toothbrush.
5. For "Balloon Games," you will need a large bag of balloons, shaving cream, a shaving razor, string, a few tacks and tape.

Story Time

"Somewhere in the depths of a humid jungle a small infantry detachment is guarding a captured meadow. On the other side, they suspect, the enemy is waiting and watching, but they haven't heard or seen anything for hours.

" 'There's probably nobody there,' one soldier suggests.

"It's beginning to get dark, and the men are getting tired, so they relax in a circle, exchanging memories about home—how long it's been, how much they miss friends and loved ones.

"Suddenly, a small but heavy object thumps on the ground a few yards away. Everyone is startled and someone shouts, 'Grenade!'

"There is no time to run for safety. The little bomb will blast any second, sparing no one. But instantly, instinctively, one soldier hurls his body on top of the grenade, muffling the explosion.

"Why did he do it? What made that soldier give his life unselfishly to save the others? What did he have to gain by it? Money? A medal? Of course not!

"The soldier who heaved himself upon that live grenade, was a special person. Jesus said, 'Greater love has no one than this, that one lay down his life for his friends.' (John 15:13, NASB). He showed one of the truest forms of love: self-sacrificial love.

"Most of us have no idea what true godly love is all about. What this man did instinctively is the type of unselfish love God wants each of us to possess. Of course, we all hope that it won't end in our giving our lives for our friends—but then, I believe God wants us to be ready to do that.

"Let me tell you of another encounter in the jungle. In January 1956, Jim Elliot and four missionary companions flew into the steaming jungle in Ecuador and landed on a stretch of sand on the edge of a river. It was a beautiful jungle, open and full of palms. But it was also a deadly jungle.

"They had come to this remote area to meet an elusive and hostile Indian tribe known as the Auca's. All of the men knew the risks they were taking. The tribe had used their spears in killing at least ten employees of the Shell Oil Company recently. This would be no easy task.

"Jim Elliot had spent a lifetime preparing for this mission. He had left the comforts of life in the United States to come to these people who had never heard of Christianity. The Auca's didn't even have a word in their vocabulary for God.

"Jim had spent six years praying for these primitive Indians. He and the missionary pilot, Nate Saint, had flown over the area and dropped gifts many times in an effort to build the trust of the natives.

"On Friday, January 6, their long awaited vigil reached a climax—they made their first contact with the Auca Indians. But it was to be a fateful encounter. On Sunday, two days later, the apparently friendly Indians suddenly turned on the missionaries and killed all five of them.

"Under normal circumstances, that might be the end to our story, but it is not. Dayuma, an Auca girl who had fled from the tribe, became a Christian through the help of Rachel Saint, sister of one of the martyred missionaries. Through Dayuma, Rachel Saint and Jim Elliot's widow, Elisabeth, were able to gain an entrance into the tribe.

"Through years of love and hard work, the Auca walls of distrust for all outsiders was finally broken and many became Christians.

"Today, the five living Auca killers have all become Christians and are leaders of the small congregation that worships near the spot where the missionaries were killed.

"What kind of love did those missionaries and their wives possess to drive them to give so much for people who were not even their friends? The only way that kind of love can be understood is from a Christian point of view. God is love and those that love God will show it by how they love their fellow men—no matter what."

Quickie Quiz

This is a simple quiz designed to lead into a discussion of how God's love differs from "human" types of love. The answers are found at the end of the questions. Read each situation, then ask your family the question and allow a moment for each to write the correct letter on his or her paper.

1. Alfred is the "weird" boy who lives down the street. He isn't good looking, he's not smart, and he's not good at sports. Most of the time, Alfred can be found doing things alone. But Alfred has a swimming pool in his backyard. Each summer, everyone tries to be Alfred's best friend. Why?"
    a. Because they feel sorry for him.
    b. Because he has a swimming pool.
    c. Because he gets better looking in the summer.
2. Ruth is mad at her little sister, Marilyn, for scribbling all over her new Bible. "Get out of my room and shut the door!" she yells. Marilyn runs out of the room and accidently slams the door on her fingers. Ruth hears her sister's scream of pain and hurries to help her. Why?
    a. She has already forgotten about the Bible.
    b. She wants to see Marilyn's bruised fingers.
    c. She cares for Marilyn even though she is mad at her.
3. Angela's older brother is a Major League baseball player. She likes to watch her brother play ball, but she's no better at playing it herself than any of the other girls. However, at school the boys always want her on their team and sometimes even makes her the captain. Usually, the boys don't even want any girls around while they're playing. Why is Angela liked by the boys?
    a. Because they like pretty girls.
    b. Because she's a good baseball player.
    c. Because her brother plays in the Major Leagues.
4. Rod and his friends ride their skateboards every

day. One afternoon they all decide to ride over to the skateboard park. But as they are getting started, Rod accidently kicks his board out from under him and it rams into the curb, breaking a wheel. Now instead of going to the park, Rod has to stay home and repair his broken wheel. "Too bad, Rod/" yell his friends as they ride on. When is Rod part of the group?
    a. When he can do what they do.
    b. All the time.
    c. When they are at the skateboard park.

"Now let's score our cards." (Discuss the correct answers with the family as you give each one. If there is disagreement, talk it out together in a positive way.) 1. b; 2. c; 3. c; 4. a.

"In most of these situations, a person has something that others like. This is how we usually are: we will be a friend to someone if they have something to offer us. This type of friendship is the selfish kind.

"In one of the situations, someone liked another person unselfishly. Do you remember which one? (2. with Ruth.) Ruth cared for her little sister even though she was angry with her at the moment. Do you think it might have been easy for Ruth to say, 'Aha! Serves you right!' when Marilyn slammed her fingers in the door?

I think so. But there was something special about Ruth. What do you think it was? (Ruth was a Christian.) Ruth gave us an example of God's love in that situation.

"People often say, 'I love you if you do this, or because you do that.' But God says, 'I love you no matter what you do!' God's love for us is an unselfish love, while all other kinds of love are human and therefore selfish. If we are Christians, we have God's Holy Spirit to help us love unselfishly."

Cartoon Time

In the Bible Activity Section there are three cartoons without captions. Have the children write what they feel are appropriate captions to make the cartoon characters show love like God would want us to.

What Is Love?

Open a Bible to 1 Corinthians 13:4-8. On a piece of paper, write a caption entitled "LOVE?" Under the heading, label two columns, "What Love Is . . ." and "What Love Isn't . . ." Go over the above passages with your family and list all of the things love is (and those which love isn't) on your paper. Once you've completed the assignment, discuss how you can "do" love.

Let's Compare

"There are many things we can compare God's love to, although there is nothing in the world that can duplicate it perfectly. We have learned that:

"God's love is like a man sacrificing his son. (Father)

"God's love is like someone dying for someone else. (Son)

"God's love is like a constant companion. (Holy Spirit)

"God's love is like a father who punishes his son." (Hebrews 12:10)

Help each family member think creatively to decide how to complete this sentence for themselves: "God's love is like—"

FAMILY FUN ACTIVITIES

Toothpaste Race

Have each member of the family get their toothbrush. Place a generous supply of toothpaste on each brush and instruct each family member that he must brush until the toothpaste drools out of the corner of his mouth. The last one to drool is the winner. When some have been disqualified, they can try to make the other's laugh.

Balloon Games

1. See who can blow up a balloon the fastest and make it pop by blowing.

2. Have a 'shave the balloon' contest. Fill balloons with either air or water. Put a generous supply of shaving cream on top of each and let your kids try their hand at "shaving" it off with a razor.

3. Try the same stunt (above) only put the balloon, filled with water, on top of a partner's head.

4. Try the balloon stomp. Tie an air-filled balloon to everyone's ankle with a piece of string. On the lawn, each family member must try to stomp everyone else's balloon while protecting his own. To make the game more interesting, tie a balloon to both ankles.

5. Have a sword fight. Place a tack through a piece of tape so that the sharp part comes through the non-sticky side. Now place the tape on the end of a long blown-up balloon. Each balloon becomes a sword. Your children must pop someone else's balloon while keeping theirs intact. Make sure you pick up the tacks after this one.

6. Have an old-fashioned water balloon fight.

Chapter Sixteen
God Is Spirit

YOUR PERSONAL PREPARATION

Introduction

In knowing God it is important to understand His substance. It is wrong to assume that since we were created in God's image (Genesis 1:27) that He occupies a physical body like we do.

Jesus said: "God is spirit" (John 4:24). That statement defines God's nature as spiritual not physical. To understand what that means you must know four things about God's spiritual substance.

First, God is immaterial—He does not possess a body. Jesus made it plain (Luke 24:39) that a spirit does not have flesh and bones. If God is spirit, He must be immaterial. But what about those expressions that represent God as having bodily parts? (i.e. "The Lord's *hand* is not so short that it cannot save; neither is His *ear* so dull that it cannot hear . . ." Isaiah 59:1 NASB). These are symbolic illustrations to bring the Infinite within our scope—they are physical pictures to make God real to us.

Second, God is invisible. The Israelites were told not to make a statue or idol of God in any form because He did not possess any form. John said, "No man has seen God at any time." Paul calls Him "the invisible God."

But what about those passages which seem to indicate that some men have seen God? R.A. Torrey said: "A man may see the reflection of his face in a glass. It would be true for the man to say, 'I saw my face,' and also, 'I never saw my face.' " So some men have seen the reflection of God's glory, but they did not see His spiritual essence. And of course, God can transform Himself into any physical form He wishes, as in the "angel of Jehovah" (Genesis 16:7-14; 22:11-18; etc.).

Third, God is alive. God is not a mere "substance," He is the living God (Psalm 84:2). Life implies feeling, power and activity. God is also the source of all life—plant, animal, human, spiritual and eternal life (Psalm 36:9).

Fourth, God is a Person. God is not a "force," He is a Person who has all of the characteristics of personality.

Spirituality is the first of God's non-moral attributes that you will be studying in the family hour. As your family comes to understand more fully the true picture of God as He is presented in the Word, they will be building a Christian foundation that will last a lifetime. Use this lesson to emphasize the spiritual nature of man and how God wants us to worship Him in Spirit.

Basic Bible Teaching

A. God is immaterial.
  1. A spirit doesn't have flesh and bones. Luke 24:39.
  2. God is spirit. John 4:24.
B. God is invisible.
  1. He is not like other "gods." Deuteronomy 4:15-19.
  2. No man can see God and live. Exodus 33:20; 1 Timothy 6:16.
  3. No man has seen God. John 1:18.
  4. He is called invisible. Romans 1:20; Colossians 1:15; 1 Timothy 1:17.
C. God is alive.
  1. He is "living." Joshua 3:10; Psalm 84:2; Matthew 16:16.
  2. He is the Source for all life. John 5:26; Psalm 36:9.
D. God is a Person.
  1. He has intellect. Exodus 3:7; Acts 15:18.
  2. He has a will. Psalm 115:3; John 6:38.
  3. He has emotional sensibility. Psalm 103:8-13; John 3:16.

Lesson Objectives

1. That the family will understand that God is spirit.
2. That the family will learn to worship God in spirit.

Things You'll Need

1. For "Skit Time," you might want to provide some props like a rubber ball, hats, etc.
2. For "Squirt Gun Games," you will need a candle and holder, squirt guns for everyone in the family, blindfolds, and shaving cream.

THE LESSON

Skit Time

The following skit is written with three parts. If you have more readers, you may want to take turns reading the different parts. The aim of this skit is to help the family members better understand the spiritual nature of God. The names "Speer" and "Ritt" were chosen to remind us of "spirit."

CHARACTERS: Speer, Ritt, and the Doctor.

(Speer is throwing a rubber ball into the air and letting it bounce.)

Speer: What are you doing?
Ritt: What does it look like?
Speer: It looks like you're throwing a ball into the air and letting it bounce.
Ritt: That's right (nonchalantly)
Speer: The ball is going up and down.
Ritt: That's very good.
Speer: What makes it go up?
Ritt: I'm throwing it up.
Speer: Of yes, I can see that.
Ritt: You have good eyes.
Speer: But what makes it go down?
Ritt: Go down?
Speer: Yes, go down. I can see that you're throwing the ball up, but I don't see you throwing it down.
Ritt: Of course not. I don't need to throw it down. It just goes down.
Speer: But what makes it go down?
Ritt: Uh, well, uh . . . I don't know.
Speer: Hey, here comes the Doctor. Let's ask him.
Doctor: Hi Speer and Ritt.
Speer: We're wondering what makes the ball go down.
Ritt: Yeah. I'm throwing it up, but I don't know what's throwing it down.
Doctor: Well, the answer is gravity.
Speer: Gravity? I don't see any gravity.
Ritt: Yeah, I can't feel it.
Speer: I can't hear it.
Ritt: I can't smell it.
Speer: I can't taste it.
Doctor: Of course not. You can't detect gravity with any of your five senses. It's invisible.
Ritt: Invisible?
Doctor: That's right.
Speer: If it's invisible, then how do you know it's there?
Doctor: Because you can see what it does. It's making your ball hit the ground.
Ritt: (Throwing the ball and watching it hit the ground.) Yeah! Gravity must be there!
Speer: Gravity works every time!
Doctor: Never fails. It's just like God.
Speer and Ritt: (Together) Like God?
Doctor: Right. Have you ever seen God?
Speer and Ritt: (Together) No.
Doctor: Neither have I because He doesn't have a body like us. But I know He's here.
Speer: How?
Doctor: Just look around.
Ritt: At what?
Doctor: At everything. Who do you think put it all together?
Speer: God?
Doctor: That's right. He made it all and He holds it all together.
Ritt: Gravity too?
Doctor: Sure. What if gravity changed its mind and decided to make everything go up instead of down?
Speer: What a mess!
Doctor: So God makes sure it does its job.
Ritt: God can do all this without a body?
Doctor: Right. The Bible says that "God is spirit."
Speer: Like a ghost?
Doctor: Yes, but not like you read in ghost stories.
Ritt: But why doesn't God just let us see Him?
Doctor: He could, if He wanted to. But He is more pleased if we believe in Him without seeing. He says in His Word that people are happy or blessed if they have not seen Him, but believe anyway.
Speer: I believe in Him because I see signs of Him everywhere.
Ritt: And the Bible tells about Him too.

A Look in the Book

"Let's turn to Genesis 1:27. We are created in God's image (or likeness). What does that mean? Do we 'look' like God? Is that God's physical image? (No.) Is it His spiritual image? (Yes.)

"God created us with a spiritual capacity. That means we have the ability to become spiritual people. Unfortunately, most people in the world never understand the spiritual part of their nature. The Christian begins to develop the spiritual dimension to life when he asks Jesus to come into his heart and life.

"Let's read 1 Corinthians 2:10-16 (in The Living Bible). As you can see in these verses, the Christian now has the Spirit of God living in His heart. We have 'a portion of the very thoughts and mind of Christ.' What a difference having God's Spirit makes in our lives!

"Now let's turn to John 4:21-24. Where are we to worship? (Jesus makes it plain here that that's not really important.) How are we to worship? (With the Holy Spirit's help.) God wants us to worship Him in Spirit—since He is Spirit. How do we do that?" (By letting God the Holy Spirit take control of our thoughts. By letting Him fill us and have first place in our lives.)

Bible Study Time

"Let's take a few moments to look up some Bible verses which tell us more about God's spiritual nature. I'll call out a different Bible reference for each one of you to read. After each of you have found your verse, we'll read and discuss them, one at a time."

1. God does not have a body.
   Luke 24:39. A Spirit does not have flesh or bones.
2. God is invisible.
   John 1:18a. No man has seen God at anytime.
3. God is alive.
   Psalm 102:27. God never grows old.
4. God is a Person.
   Psalm 103:8-13. God has emotions and sensibilities.

Hidden Words

The block of letters in the Bible Activity Section contains ten words that relate to this week's program. They may be found across, down or diagonally. The words are: "Spirit, invisible, person, alive, spiritual, worship, truth, God, Christ and holy." If your children are younger, you may have to tell them what the words are so that they will know what to look for.

FAMILY FUN ACTIVITIES

Squirt Gun Games

Light a candle and time the different members of the family as they put it out with the use of a squirt gun. Once everyone has had a try, play the same game again, only this time blindfold each contestant.

Another possibility is to divide the family into teams of two. One person has some shaving cream on his nose. The other is blindfolded and given the squirt gun. He must shoot off the shaving cream by listening to his partner's instructions.

A good finale to these games is to have a good old-fashioned squirt gun fight.

Chapter Seventeen
God Is Unlimited

YOUR PERSONAL PREPARATION

Introduction

God is bigger and wiser by far than any conception we may have of Him. The Bible teaches us that He is unlimited in every way. Therefore it is impossible for us to fully comprehend these characteristics, because we are limited beings—and our minds can only compute so much!

Although this lesson is designed to help us get a "handle" on how big and unlimited God really is, we must ultimately accept God's knowledge, size, power and presence by faith. As Christians we can rejoice in the fact that His unlimitedness is used on our behalf.

The concept that God is unlimited is taught here in three parts. God is omniscient (all-knowing), omnipotent (all-powerful), and He is omnipresent (everywhere present).

Because God's unlimitedness can best be summarized by a look into the evening sky, this lesson is designed to be given at night. Keep this in mind as you prepare for this week's family hour.

Basic Bible Teaching

A. God is omniscient (all-knowing).
   1. He knows our thoughts. Psalm 94:11; 139:2.
   2. He knows our hearts. Psalm 44:21; Acts 15:8.
   3. He knows our sins. Psalm 69:5.
   4. He knows our needs. Matthew 6:8.
   5. He knows all about us. Matthew 10:30.
   6. He knows all things. Psalm 139:4; 1 John 3:20.
B. God is omnipotent (all-powerful).
   1. Everything is possible with Him. Matthew 19:26.
   2. He can do what men cannot. Luke 18:27.
   3. All power belongs to Him. Psalm 68:34.
C. God is omnipresent (everywhere present).
   1. He is always with us. Psalm 139:7; Matthew 28:20; Hebrews 13:5.
   2. He is past, present, and future. Revelation 1:8.

Lesson Objectives

1. That the family will understand that God knows everything.
2. That the family will understand that God can do anything.
3. That the family will understand that God is always present.
4. That the family will realize that we can trust in God because He uses these attributes for our benefit.

Things You'll Need

1. For "Coloring Time," you'll need crayons or colored pencils.
2. For "Family Fun Activities," you should have a small telescope (rent, borrow or buy one) and a good star guidebook.

THE LESSON

Story Time

"Have you ever tried to hide something from God? Have you ever doubted that God could do something? Have you ever thought He couldn't hear you when you needed Him? Well, there once lived a man who felt that way. His name was Jonah, and one day God came to him with a job to do.

" 'Go to the city of Ninevah,' said the Lord, 'and tell them that because they are so wicked, I am going to destroy their whole city.'

"But Jonah didn't want to go, so he decided to go—the other way. He went to the harbor and bought passage on a ship going in the opposite direction, to Tarshish. Boarding the ship, Jonah hid deep in the dark hold. Can you believe that? Jonah thought he could hide from God.

"Soon the ship was under sail and ran into an extremely violent storm. The crew feared for their lives and began to cry out to their false gods for help.

"The captain of the vessel went down into the hold and found Jonah—sleeping! 'What are you doing down here?' He shouted. 'Don't you know the danger we're in? Get up and cry to your God for help!'

"The superstitious crew got together to draw straws to discover who had made the gods angry. Since Jonah drew the shortest lot, they assumed he must be the offender.

" 'Who are you,' they wanted to know, 'and where are you from?'

"Jonah replied, 'I am a Jew, and my God is the true God. I was trying to run away from Him, but I guess it didn't work. He knew where I was all the time.'

" 'That was a dumb thing to do!' they shouted at him, angrily. 'Now what are we going to do to stop this storm?'

" 'You'll have to throw me overboard,' Jonah said. 'I know that my sin is the cause of this storm.'

"At first they didn't want to do it. But as the storm got worse, they decided they had no choice. So they picked Jonah up and tossed him into the sea.

"Suddenly, the storm stopped! The crew gave glory to Jonah's God, realizing what a powerful God He really is!

"God's power that day didn't stop with weather. He caused a great fish to come and swallow Jonah—hook, line and sinker! The prophet spent three days and nights in the fish's belly.

"Poor old Jonah started crying out to God. And of course the Lord heard him because He was right there with the prophet. Jonah was miserable. He promised the Lord that he would never worship anyone else. So God ordered the giant fish to spit the prophet out, and the fish spit him onto the beach—right where Jonah had started from!

"Once again, the Lord told Jonah to go to Nineveh and warn the people of their coming destruction. This time Jonah obeyed. He went to the city and declared to the crowds that in forty days God was going to destroy them because of their sin.

"Much to Jonah's surprise, the people listened to him. They decided to repent of their sin and began to worship the Lord. When God saw how completely the people had changed, He decided not to destroy them after all.

"The Lord's decision angered Jonah. 'I knew you would do that, Lord!' he cried 'I knew that because of your mercy you would forgive them and not destroy them after all! That's why I ran away the first time! (Jonah was making excuses for himself.) Now you've made me into a liar! Why don't you just kill me? I'd rather be dead than alive!'

"The Lord scolded Jonah for his selfishness. God is much more interested in 120,000 souls, He said, than He is in pleasing one selfish man."

Application

"In the story of Jonah, God shows us His great power. How do we see His great knowledge? (God knew where Jonah was hiding.) How did he show His great power? (God caused a terrible storm and ordered a giant fish to swallow Jonah and spit him out.) We also learned that God is everywhere. How? (God was even in the giant fish with Jonah.)

"Nothing is too much for God to know or do. There is no place God cannot go. The Bible tells us that the Lord knows what we are thinking and doing at all times. He knows everything we need. He knows all there is to know about us—even the number of hairs on our head!

"We know from the Bible that everything is possible with God. He can do anything, even things men cannot do, no matter how hard they try! In fact, God is the owner of all power—it all belongs to Him! The Bible also tells us that God is everywhere. Therefore, we can never get away from Him. God is even in places that man has never been! He has promised to be with us always and never leave us. (See "Basic Bible Teaching" for references.)

"See what a great God we have? Since He knows everything, can do everything, and is everywhere, we can put our trust in Him. We never need to worry about anything that happens to us no matter how terrible, because God knows about us and will take care of us, no matter where we are."

Coloring Time

Have the children put the correct title on each of the three drawings of Jonah in the Bible Activity Section. Have them put the captions "God Shows His Power," "God Is Everywhere" and "God Knows Everything" on the correct drawings. Next, have the children color the drawings of Jonah and his experiences.

Star Gaze

Take the family out into the backyard to look at the stars. Try to communicate the immense size of the universe.

The sun is 93 million miles from us. The closest star is 4 light years away. A light year is the distance light travels in one year at 186,000 miles per second. To figure out how many miles are in a light year, have an older teenager multiply:

186,000		(the number of miles light travels in one second)
x	60	(the number of seconds in a minute)
x	60	(the number of minutes in an hour)
x	24	(the number of hours in a day)
x365.25		(the days in a year)

TOTAL: Almost 6 trillion miles; 6,000,000,000,000! That's one light year!

Although the nearest star is 4 light years away, it would take *100,000 light years* to cross our galaxy, the Milky Way! And that's not the end of space! Some of those "stars" are not stars at all, but galaxies the size of our Milky Way. They are so far away from us they just look like stars.

And think about this: if God made all of this, He has to be much bigger than the huge universe which He has created. "Lord, in the beginning you made the earth, and the heavens are the work of your hands. They will disappear into nothingness, but you will remain forever. They will become worn out like old clothes, and some day you will fold them up and replace them. But you yourself will never change, and your years will never end" (Hebrews 1:10-12, TLB).

How Much Are You Worth?

Go inside and read Psalm 8 from The Living Bible. Point out how small we are in relationship to the universe. How is it that God could care for us?

"If we could build a giant scale and place the entire universe on one tray, what could we possibly put on the other tray to make it balance up?

"One soul. That's right. One human soul, one life is worth much more to God than the entire universe. Jesus said, 'For what will a man be profited if he gains the whole world (or cosmos—the universe) and loses or forfeits his own soul?' (Matthew 16:26, NASB). Even the entire universe is not worth more than one human life to God.

"Isn't it exciting to know that we have such a big unlimited God who cares so much for us? Let's thank God, right now, for His unlimitedness. Let's thank Him that He has an unlimited love for us."

FAMILY FUN ACTIVITIES

If you own a small telescope or can borrow or rent one, go back out into the backyard and spend some time looking at the different stars and planets in the sky. A good star guidebook will also help you find and explain what you are viewing.

Chapter Eighteen
God Is Perfect and Unchanging

YOUR PERSONAL PREPARATION

Introduction

When we look into the Old Testament it is easy for us to assume that God has changed. The Law, the Ten Commandments and the sacrificial system didn't make man follow after God. So we reason, God is now trying a new method—the cross of Christ.

Although God has dealt differently with men in various periods of history, His nature does not and cannot change. He did not make a mistake when He gave the Law; it still adequately reveals God's character and standard. Jesus said He did not come to destroy this standard but rather to fulfill it.

We must always be wary of trying to understand God with our human reasoning. God is perfect and He never makes mistakes—this we cannot truly comprehend because we are sinful and imperfect.

God has no beginning or end; He does not change. Again, the human mind can never fully grasp this concept. Almost everything we know has a beginning or ending. Everything seems to change, decay, rust or grow old and die.

Even though we have human limitations in understanding God's nature, it is important to your family's spiritual well-being that they grasp God's perfection and unchangeableness.

If they think of God as imperfect or subject to change, they will have a foundation of sand upon which to build their Christianity and ultimately their lives. If their God has flaws, their faith will eventually tumble like a sand castle.

Help your family understand that God is perfect and thus we can trust Him never to make a mistake. Help them see that God never changes, thus we know that our future is secure. It is a good feeling to know that you are in the hands of a perfect, wise and changeless God.

Basic Bible Teaching

A. God's perfection
  1. God is perfect. Psalm 18:30.
  2. The Father is perfect. Matthew 5:48.
  3. Jesus is holy, innocent, undefiled and separated from sinners (sin). Hebrews 7:26.
  4. Jesus is sinless. 1 Peter 2:21-25.
  5. Jesus is perfect. Hebrews 7:28.
  6. God's will is perfect. Romans 12:2.
  7. God gives perfect and good gifts. James 1:17.
  8. God's Word is perfect. James 1:25.

B. God's Immutability (Unchangeableness)
  1. God was never born. Psalm 102:24-27.
  2. God will never die. Psalm 90:2.
  3. God does not vary. 1 Timothy 1:17.
  4. God is eternal. Psalm 102:27.
  5. God does not change. Malachi 3:6; Hebrews 6:17.
  6. Jesus Christ is always the same. Hebrews 13:8.
  7. God's unchangeableness consists in the fact that He will always respond the same (based on His moral nature) to our variations in character and conduct. See 2 Chronicles 7:14.

Lesson Objectives

1. That your family will come to understand that God is perfect and, as such, He never makes mistakes.

2. That your family will come to understand that God never changes and, as such, our eternal destiny is secure.

3. That your family will trust in God as their all-wise and loving Father.

Things You'll Need

For "Praise God with Music," pull out any musical instruments in the family to use to praise God.

THE LESSON

Learn from the Circle

In the Bible Activity Section there is a drawing of a circle. Cut it out and hold it up while you discuss God's perfectness and eternity with your family.

"You can see that I'm holding a piece of paper which has on it a perfect circle. This circle is just like God, in two ways. A circle has no beginning or end. No matter how many times you travel around it, you still have just as far to go as when you began.

"God is like this circle; He has no beginning and no end. He has always existed and He always will exist. Let's read the first verse that's printed inside the circle.

"There's a second way this circle is like God; it is perfect. God has no flaws; He never makes mistakes.

He is perfect, just like this circle is perfectly round. Let's read the second verse printed inside the circle.

"Whenever you see a circle, try to think of God. And remember, just like a circle, God is perfect and unchangeable." (At this point you might want to have your younger children color circles of their own.)

Bible Drill

For a few minutes, have a quick Bible drill. See who can find the verse first. Have the family read each verse, then discuss what it tells us about God's perfectness and unchangeableness.

>Matthew 5:48.
>Hebrews 7:26.
>Hebrews 7:28.
>1 Timothy 1:17.
>Psalm 90:2.
>Malachi 3:6.
>Hebrews 6:17.

Does God ever Make Mistakes?

If you have teenagers who have experienced major or minor tragedies which have caused them to doubt whether God is really perfect, you will want to deal with this issue. Even if your children have no problem in this area, it is a good idea to build a foundation now so that they will have no problems in the future.

"I'm going to share four examples. You tell me if God has made a mistake in each one.

1. "A friend or loved one dies unexpectedly, maybe in an accident."
2. "A new war begins in the Far East."
3. "A baby is born with a defect."
4. "Someone is murdered."

"God allows everything that happens on our earth. He has allowed things like those I've just mentioned. Did He make any mistakes? (No.) In every situation mentioned, God has allowed someone else to make a mistake. God tells us what is right in His Book, and expects us to do it. But if we want to sin—He gives us the freedom to do it.

"All of the tragedy in the world is the result of sin. The wages of sin is death. If there was no sin in the world, there would also be no death. The same is true for physical and mental defects—they would not exist, if it wasn't for the presence of sin. (In the Old Testament no animal with a physical defect could be offered as a sacrifice to God as they were considered symbolic of a sinful condition.) Even nature suffers as a result of the sin that is in the world. Let's read Romans 8:19-23:

" 'For all creation is waiting patiently and hopefully for that future day when God will resurrect his children. For on that day thorns and thistles, sin, death, and decay—the things that overcame the world against its will at God's command—will all disappear, and the world around us will share in the glorious freedom from sin which God's children enjoy.

" 'For we know that even the things of nature, like animals and plants, suffer in sickness and death as they await this great event. And even we Christians, although we have the Holy Spirit within us as a foretaste of future glory, also groan to be released from pain and suffering. We, too, wait anxiously for that day when God will give us our full rights as his children, including the new bodies he has promised us—bodies that will never be sick again and will never die' (TLB).

"So, the world suffers because of its own sin. God has not made a mistake; He has simply allowed men to sin if they so desire.

"Christians, of necessity, also suffer because of the sin in the world. But, praise the Lord, God has promised not to let anything happen to us that is not His will." (Read Romans 8:28.)

Learning to Give Thanks

"If God has promised to make everything that comes into our lives 'work to the good' then we need to learn how to give thanks for everything that happens to us.

"Let's read 1 Thessalonians 5:18 together." (Emphasize the importance of each word in the verse.)

"What should we give thanks for—everything. Let's start giving thanks for everything we can think of that God has given to us—even the things we don't like."

Have a time of prayer (possibly with your eyes open) on a conversational level, and thank God for everything you can possibly think of.

Praise God with Music

If you have any musical instruments in the family, pull them out and use them to give glory to God after reading Psalm 150 together. Have a time of praise, singing and making melody to God in your hearts.

If you do not have a "musically-inclined" family, play a cut or two from a Christian record album of praise and just sing along. The key to a good time of praise is to get into God. This cannot be done if anyone feels "funny" about singing at home or is struggling with the words or tune. It might be a good idea to play the same praise song two or three times (or choose one that is repetitious) so that everyone can lose themselves in the message of the song and sing with feeling.

Treasure Hunt

In the Bible Activity Section there is a Treasure Hunt. Have the family look up each treasure reference and record the correct "treasure quality" in the spaces provided on the Treasure Hunt page.

FAMILY FUN ACTIVITIES

Fun With Bible Riddles

The following riddles from the Bible should help liven up your family fun time.

1. "Who is the shortest man in the Bible?" (Answer: "Bildad the Shuhite.")

2. "What did Adam and Eve do after God made them leave the Garden of Eden?" (Answer: "Raised Cain.")

.3. "Who was Jonah's tutor?" (Answer: "The fish that brought him up.")

4. "Why did the great fish cough up Jonah?" (Answer: "You just can't keep a good man down.")

5. "Why was Moses the most wicked man who ever lived?" (Answer: "He broke the Ten Commandments all at once.")

6. "How many pairs of animals did Moses bring aboard the ark?" (Answer: "None. Moses didn't go aboard the ark; Noah did.")

7. "How do you know Noah had a pig aboard the ark?" (Answer: "He had Ham.")

8. "What is the first biblical prediction about the coming of television?" (Answer: " 'Now we see through a glass darkly.' ")

9. "Do you know what the name of Isaiah's horse was?" (Answer: "Is me. He said, 'Woe, is me.' ")

10. "Where was deviled ham first mentioned in the Bible?" (Answer: "When the demons entered the swine.")

Family Favorites

Let the family select their favorite game from past family hour times.

Answers to crossword puzzle Chapter 5 page 67

Fellowship

1A	Body	1D	Continue
2A	One	2D	You
3A	Not	3D	We
4A	Him	4D	Loved
5A	Purified	5D	Light
6A	Brother	6D	Is
7A	Heart	7D	Abides
8A	Praise	8D	Members

Answers to crossword puzzle Chapter 10 page 73

The Names of Jesus

ACROSS
1. Immanuel
2. Omega
3. Savior
4. Jesus
5. Door
6. Healer
7. Light
8. Man
9. Christ
10. He
11. Creator
12. Branch
13. Vine

DOWN
14. Alpha
15. Bread
10. High
7. Life
16. Lamb
17. Messiah
18. Master
19. Son
20. I Am
21. Lord
22. Priest
23. Way
24. Maker (He makes)
25. Nazarene

Bible Activity Section

BIBLE BASKETBALL

The following Bible basketball questions are designed to help you have a comprehensive review of the material you have presented during your last eighteen family hour times. The questions have been designed both for younger children and older teenagers.

Divide your family into two teams. Each team gets to answer one question on each round. The answering player can choose a "free throw" (for one point), a "field goal" (for two), and a "three-point play" (for three). A quarter consists of ten questions. Five for each side. If you have two or more players on a side, make certain you alternate back and forth so that each player gets the same number of questions.

The free throws are the more simple questions designed for your younger children. If your family is divided because of age differences and you cannot make the teams completely even, you may want to add some rules which will make things even. For example, the younger children can have an extra free throw if they make the first one. Or, penalize the older children by having them lose points if they miss their questions and restrict them to two- and three-point questions.

Keep a running score and score by quarters on the sheet provided for this purpose in the Bible Activity Section.

FREE THROWS (For One Point Each)
1. Does God ever make mistakes? (No.)
2. Who was swallowed by the big fish? (Jonah.)
3. Is anything possible with God? (Yes.)
4. Is God merely a "force"? (No. He is a Person.)
5. Is God a Spirit? (Yes.)
6. Most of the love you hear about today in popular songs is really not true love at all in the Christian sense. True or False? (True.)
7. What were the names of the first two people in the world? (Adam and Eve.)
8. Who tempted Eve? (The serpent—who was Satan in disguise.)
9. God is perfectly just most of the time. True or false? (False. God is just all of the time.)
10. Who asked to see God in the Old Testament? (Moses.)
11. Is light really white? (No. It is a composite of different colors.)
12. Does the Old Testament teach that God is plural in personality? (Yes.)
13. Is the Holy Spirit God? (Yes.)
14. Is Jesus God? (Yes.)
15. How many fathers do you have? (Two).
16. Name the three members of the Trinity. (Father, Son and Holy Spirit.)
17. Who became a Christian while he was on the road to Damascus? (Paul.)
18. What did God save Daniel from? (Lions.)
19. Who was Abraham's son? (Isaac.)
20. Is church attendance important? (Yes.)
21. How do we talk to God? (Prayer.)
22. What is God's Word called? (The Bible, Scriptures, etc.)
23. Who invented the Morse Code? (Samuel Morse.)
24. What page in the Wordless Book stands for sin? (Black one.)
25. How do you know that God loves you? (John 3:16; the Bible tells us; etc. Use your judgment here.)
26. Can we get to God without going through the Lord Jesus? (No. John 14:6.)
27. Who was Simon Peter's brother? (Andrew.)

FIELD GOALS (For Two Points Each)

1. What disciple introduced his brother to Jesus? (Andrew.)
2. What is the wages of sin? (Death. Romans 6:23.)
3. What did Derek do in the story we had about sin? (He stole a fruit pie.)
4. What was prayer compared to in our lesson? (C.B. Radio.)
5. The early church prayed for a Christian who was put in prison. An angel let him out while they were praying. Who was he? (Peter.)
6. When you stimulate one another to love and good deeds, what are you practicing? (Fellowship.)
7. Can fellowship happen outside of the church? (Yes.)
8. It's impossible to please God without what? (Faith.)
9. Who was willing to sacrifice his son for God? (Abraham.)
10. What's another word for faith? (Trust.)

11. Why didn't Abraham sacrifice his son? (An angel stopped him.)

12. Why did Daniel get thrown into the lion's den? (He broke a law against praying.)

13. Who was the greatest Christian missionary of all time? (Paul.)

14. Who sent Jesus to earth? (The Father.)

15. What title of Jesus' means "God with us"? (Immanuel.)

16. What is the Old Testament name for "Christ." (Messiah.)

17. Name three different titles or names of Christ. (Jesus, the Son, Christ, Messiah, Lord, Master, etc.)

18. Name two things the Holy Spirit does. (Indwells us, fills us, convicts us of sin, gives spiritual gifts, seals, comforts, etc.)

19. Who prays for us? (The Holy Spirit.)

20. What is God's first and foremost moral quality? (Holiness.)

21. Why did Isaiah feel that He was unclean in His vision of God? (He was sinful and God is holy.)

22. Which of the following is not a moral character quality of God's? Holiness, justice, mercy, being everywhere at once, love, truth. (Being everywhere is not a moral quality.)

23. God provides for us a pardon for our sins through ____? (Through Christ's death on the cross.)

24. How many missionaries were martyred in the jungles of Ecuador by the Auca Indians? (Five.)

25. What happened to the Auca Indian killers of those missionairies? (They all became Christians.)

26. Invisible best describes what characteristic of God? (The fact that He is a Spirit.)

27. Where is God? (Everywhere.)

28. What does God know about? (He knows about everything.)

29. Why didn't Jonah want to go to Nineveh? (He was afraid the Lord would save them and make Jonah a liar.)

30. When was God born? (He was never born; He has always existed.)

THREE-POINT PLAYS (For Three Points Each)

1. How is the circle like God (It is perfect and it never ends.)

2. How big is a light year? (Six trillion years long.)

3. Tell how the story of Jonah reveals God's three unlimited attributes? (God was all-knowing because He knew where Jonah was hiding. He was all-powerful in that He sent a storm and a great fish to swallow Jonah. He was everywhere in that He was in the fish to hear Jonah's prayer.)

4. Name two things that love is, according to 1 Corinthians 13. (Patient, kind, not boastful, etc. Look up the passage to double-check any answer given.)

5. The highest form of human love is what? (Self-sacrificial love.)

6. Quote 1 Peter 1:15, 16. (Look it up to be certain the answer is correct.)

7. Quote Ephesians 5:18. (Again, look it up.)

8. What is the Old Testament name for "Christ? (Messiah.)

9. Give one verse of Scripture that tells that Jesus is God? (John 1:1; 20:28; Hebrews 1:8; etc. Use your own judgment on the answer to this question.)

10. How many books did the apostle Paul write? (At least 13, maybe 14.)

11. Quote Isaiah 40:8.

12. How many chapters of the Bible did Haralan Popov memorize in prison? (Forty-seven!)

13. According to Romans 10:9, 10, salvation involves what two things? (Confession with your mouth that Jesus is Lord and belief in your heart that God has raised Jesus from the dead.)

14. Jonas was whose father? (Peter and Andrew.)

Chapter 1   **Keys To The Kingdom**

KEYS TO THE KINGDOM

- I TIMOTHY 2:5
- JOHN 10:10b
- JOHN 3:16
- ROMANS 10:9, 10

Chapter 3   **Learning The Morse Code**

THE MORSE CODE

A •—	J •———	S •••
B —•••	K —•—	T —
C —•—•	L •—••	U ••—
D —••	M ——	V •••—
E •	N —•	W •——
F ••—•	O ———	X —••—
G ——•	P •——•	Y —•——
H ••••	Q ——•—	Z ——••
I ••	R •—•	

PROBLEM ONE: Write the correct letter below the symbol.

"• •••   •   •—•   —•—••

•——   ———   •—•   —••

———   ••—•   ——•   ——••

—•—•   •—•   ———   •••—   •   •••

—   •—•   ••—   • "

Proverbs 30:5b TLB

PROBLEM TWO: Write the correct letter below the symbol.

"—•—   —• ———   •—•

•——   ••••   •—•   —   ••••   ••   •••

—•—   •   •—•   •—••

••   •—   —•—•   •••

•—   —•   —••

——   •   •—   —•   •••"

2 Timothy 2:15b TLB

PROBLEM THREE: Write the correct letter below the symbol.

"—•••   •—••   •   •••   •••   —••

•—••   ———   •—•   —••

•—   —•—   —•—•—   ••••

——   •   •—•—   —•—•—   ••—   •—•

•—••   ••   •—••   •   •••"

Psalm 119:12 TLB

59

Chapter 2 — God's Love

1st PRINCIPLE OF GOD'S LOVE

God Loves You and Has the Heaviest Life Style for You

Jesus said: "I have come that you might have and enjoy life, and have it in abundance—to the full, till it overflows."
—(John 10:10b Amp.)

Jesus cares like nobody else. He wants you to get the most out of your life. He alone knows what's happening. He will never disappoint you. He can always be trusted to give you the best.

But the reason we don't experience this LOVE is because:

Sin is simply not doing what God wants. It's rebelling. If this barrier continues, it will result in spiritual death.

"The wages of sin is death, but the gift of God is eternal life through Jesus Christ our Lord." —(Romans 6:23)

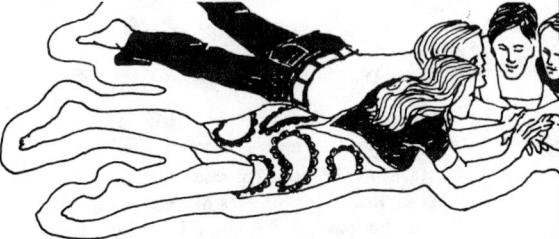

You are Now in the Family:
If you have personally asked Jesus into your life, "you are now one of God's children, a Son of God." (1 John 4:1)

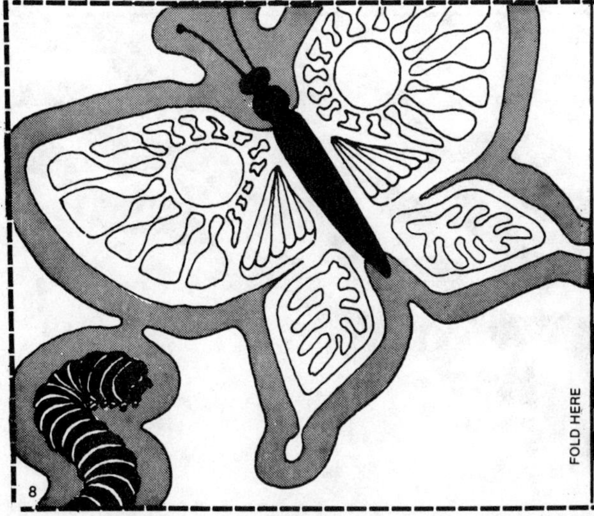

"These things I have written to you who believe in the name of the Son of God (Jesus), in order that you may know that you have eternal life." --(1 John 5:13)

© 1978 John C. Souter

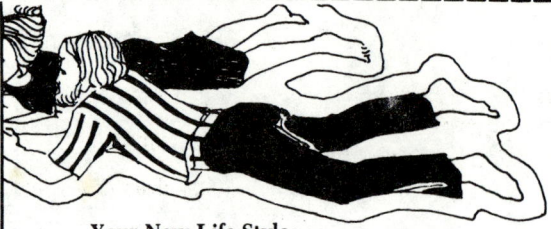

Your New Life Style:
1. Learn to depend on Jesus. (Colossians 2:6, 1 Peter 5:7)
2. Read your Bible—it is God's Word. (2 Timothy 3:16)
3. Talk to God by prayer. (Philippians 4:6, Matthew 21:22)
4. Get together with your other brothers and sisters in Christ and learn more about Jesus (Hebrews 10:25, 1 John 1:3)

2nd PRINCIPLE OF GOD'S LOVE

We've All Ignored God and Have Built a Barrier Called Sin

The Book says that "we have all sinned and have fallen short of the glory of God." —(Romans 3:23)

4th PRINCIPLE OF GOD'S LOVE

Jesus is Waiting to Come Into Your Life

He wants to show you God's love and remove the barrier we have created.

"I stand at the door (of your heart) and knock; if any man hears My voice and opens the door, I will come in to him and sup with him and he with Me."

Right now you can find that Free Love from God by prayer. Talk to God right now and say something like this:

"Lord Jesus, thank you for dying for my sins. Please come into my heart and make me the kind of person you want me to be. Thank You for coming in and giving me Your free love gift."

3rd PRINCIPLE OF GOD'S LOVE

Jesus Christ is the Only One Who Can Remove This Barrier

The Bible tells us that: "God demonstrates His love for us in that while we were yet sinners, Christ died for us." (Romans 5:8)

Jesus is the only way: "I am the way, the truth and the life, no one comes to the Father except by Me." (John 14:6)

Chapter 3   **Sing Along**

Look up Psalm 119: 12-10 and answer the questions on the right.

5 to 10 minutes.   Date _____

Psalm number _____

1. What does this Psalm talk about?

   [ ] A call for judgment   [ ] Praising God

   [ ] Sorrow over sin   [ ] Thanksgiving

   [ ] Prayer for help   [ ] Other _____

2. Copy the verse you like best: _____
_____
_____
_____

3. What does this Psalm say to me? _____
_____
_____
_____

Look up Psalm 119: 101-106 and answer the questions on the right.

5 to 10 minutes.   Date _____

Psalm number _____

1. What does this Psalm talk about?

   [ ] A call for judgment   [ ] Praising God

   [ ] Sorrow over sin   [ ] Thanksgiving

   [ ] Prayer for help   [ ] Other _____

2. Copy the verse you like best: _____
_____
_____
_____

3. What does this Psalm say to me? _____
_____
_____
_____

SING ALONG

Chapter 3   **I Read My Bible!**

I Read My Bible!	I Read My Bible!	I Read My Bible!	I Read My Bible!
NAME _____	NAME _____	NAME _____	NAME _____
WEEK _____	WEEK _____	WEEK _____	WEEK _____
☐ Sunday	☐ Sunday	☐ Sunday	☐ Sunday
☐ Monday	☐ Monday	☐ Monday	☐ Monday
☐ Tuesday	☐ Tuesday	☐ Tuesday	☐ Tuesday
☐ Wednesday	☐ Wednesday	☐ Wednesday	☐ Wednesday
☐ Thursday	☐ Thursday	☐ Thursday	☐ Thursday
☐ Friday	☐ Friday	☐ Friday	☐ Friday
☐ Saturday	☐ Saturday	☐ Saturday	☐ Saturday

Chapter 4   **I Prayed Today!**

I Prayed Today!	I Prayed Today!	I Prayed Today!	I Prayed Today!
NAME _____	NAME _____	NAME _____	NAME _____
WEEK _____	WEEK _____	WEEK _____	WEEK _____
☐ Sunday	☐ Sunday	☐ Sunday	☐ Sunday
☐ Monday	☐ Monday	☐ Monday	☐ Monday
☐ Tuesday	☐ Tuesday	☐ Tuesday	☐ Tuesday
☐ Wednesday	☐ Wednesday	☐ Wednesday	☐ Wednesday
☐ Thursday	☐ Thursday	☐ Thursday	☐ Thursday
☐ Friday	☐ Friday	☐ Friday	☐ Friday
☐ Saturday	☐ Saturday	☐ Saturday	☐ Saturday

Chapter 5

Crossword Puzzle

"Fellowship"

"A" stands for "Across" and "D" stands for "Down." Look up each verse and place the missing word in the blanks. Use **New American Standard Version**. (Answers on Page 56.)

"But now there are many members, but one ___(1A)___." 1 Cor. 12:20.

"Beloved, if God so loved us, we also ought to love ___(2A)___ another." 1 John 4:11.

"For the body is ___(3A)___ member, but many." 1 Cor. 12:14.

"And this commandment we have from ___(4A)___, that the one who loves God should love his brother also." 1 John 4:21.

"Since you have in obedience to the truth ___(5A)___ your souls for a sincere love of the brethren, fervently love one another from the heart." 1 Peter 1:22.

"The one who says he is in the light and yet hates his ___(6A)___ is in the darkness until now." 1 John 2:9.

"This is My commandment, that ___(2D)___ love one another, just as I have ___(4D)___ you." John 15:12.

"Praise the Lord! I will give thanks to the Lord with all my ___(7A)___, in the company of the upright and in the assembly." Psalm 111:1.

"Let them extol Him also in the congregation of the people, and ___(8A)___ Him at the seat of the elders." Psalm 107:32.

"Let love of the brethren ___(1D)___." Hebrews 13:1.

"___(3D)___ know that ___(3D)___ have passed out of death into life, because we love the brethren." 1 John 3:14.

"...but if we walk in the light as He Himself is in the ___(5D)___, we have fellowship with one another, and the blood of Jesus, His Son, cleanses us from all sin." 1 John 1:7.

"The one who loves his brother ___(7D)___ in the light and there is no cause for stumbling in him." 1 John 2:10.

"For even as the body ___(6D)___ one and yet has many members, and all the members of the body, though they are many, are one body, so also ___(6D)___ Christ." 1 Cor. 12:12.

"Now you are Christ's body, and individually ___(8D)___ of it." 1 Cor. 12:27.

Chapter 7   "Trial Briefs" & "Telegram"

TRIAL BRIEF FOR DEFENSE

Emphasize the following points:
1. Daniel has obeyed a higher law given by God—therefore he is innocent.
2. Human laws only have real authority when the enternal God approves of them.
3. This is a bad law. Even our ruler agrees that this is a bad law.
4. Every God-fearing person (Christian) has the responsibility to disobey any man-made law that violates God's will and His Word.
5. Daniel has obviously obeyed every other law of the kingdom. His character declares that he would not willingly disobey a just law.
6. Daniel could have closed his curtains and no one would have known about his prayers. This only reveals we are dealing with a man of the highest personal character and integrity.
7. This law violates every person's God-given right to worship as he sees fit. Therefore, if Daniel is guilty, he is guilty of breaking a law that should never have come into existence.

TRIAL BRIEF FOR PROSECUTION

Emphasize the following points:
1. Daniel didn't obey the law.
2. Daniel had wholesale disregard for the law.
3. The law is more important than any individual person.
4. Who is Daniel that he thinks he is above the law?
5. The ruler of our nation signed this law and it cannot be changed.
6. The ruler of our kingdom certainly knows what he is doing.
7. Doesn't Daniel realize that everyone obeys this law but him?
8. There are many gods in this kingdom. Does Daniel think his God is the only one?
9. If we accept the fact that Daniel is guiltless because he "obeyed a higher law," where will it all end? Soon everyone will claim that to avoid obeying the law.

WESTERN UNION TELEGRAM

_____
_____
_____
_____
_____
_____
_____
_____

Chapter 8   "Business Cards" & "Man Hunt" Bible Study

"Man Hunt" Bible Study: Study the entire life of Daniel as it is given in the Bible. Read the book of Daniel, chapters 1 to 6, in **The Living Bible** and then answer all the questions on the "Man Hunt" form at right.

MANHUNT

15 to 20 minutes.   Date _____

Man You Are Hunting: _____

1. What he (she) did for a living: _____

2. His background (family, ancestors, friends, when and where he lived): _____

3. A summary of his life: _____

4. Important events in his life: _____

5. His relationship with God: _____

6. What can I learn from his life? _____

Ambassador
_____
(Character Slogan)
For Christ
2 CORINTHIANS 5:20

_____
(Character Slogan)

Representing The:

King of Kings

Revelation 19:16

Member of the:

GOD SQUAD

_____
(Character Slogan)

Ready always to give an answer about the Faith. 1 Peter 3:15

Chapter 10

Crossword Puzzle

"The Names Of Jesus"
Use **New American Standard** version.

ACROSS

1. Name which means "God with us." (Matthew 1:23).
2. Name which means "the last." (Revelation 1:8).
3. Name which takes away our sin. (Luke 2:11).
4. Christ's given name. (Matthew 1:21).
5. Symbolic name for an entrance way. (John 10:9).
6. Miracle worker. (Matthew 4:23).
7. The One who illuminates (John 8:12).
8. Jesus' humanity. (Phil. 2:8).
9. New Testament name for Messiah. (Matthew 16:16).
10. A pronoun used for Jesus. (Matt. 1:21).
11. He made the world. (Col. 1:16, 1 Peter 4:19).
12. Old Testament term that is part of a tree. (Zechariah 3:8).
13. New Testament term that is part of a plant. (John 15:1).

DOWN

14. Name which means "the beginning." (Rev. 1:8).
15. He is the _____ of life. (John 6:48).
10. The kind of priest Jesus is. (Hebrews 9:11).
7. Jesus is the Way, Truth, and _____ . (John 14:6).
16. A spotless and pure animal sacrifice. (John 1:29).
17. The Old Testament term for Christ. (Daniel 9:26).
18. The One in control. (Luke 5:5).
19. His relationship with the Father. (John 5:20).
20. His claim to oneness with the Father (two words). (John 8:58).
21. Another term for "sir." (Mark 2:28).
22. He intercedes. (Hebrews 9:11).
23. He is how we get to heaven. (John 14:6).
24. One who makes. (Jer. 10:16).
25. Known by His home town. (Matt. 2:23).

(Answers on Page 56.)

73

Chapter 12 — "Trinity" & "Mysterious Dots"

THE TRINITY

THE SON is not is not HOLY is not FATHER is is is GOD HOLY SPIRIT is not FATHER

MYSTERIOUS DOTS

Chapter 13 — "Decode the Verses"

BUT BE HOLY NOW IN EVERYTHING YOU DO, JUST AS THE LORD IS HOLY, WHO INVITED YOU TO BE HIS CHILD.
1 PETER 1:15 TLB

HE HIMSELF HAS SAID, "YOU MUST BE HOLY, FOR I AM HOLY."
1 PETER 1:16 TLB

Chapter 15 — "Cartoon Time"

75

Chapter 16 & 18 — "Hidden Words" & "The Circle"

HIDDEN WORDS

```
Z I N V I S I B L E
Q U I W L P V J W U
U R V P O I Z M Q N
B G O C H R S J T O
T G U T H I I J L S
H B C E S T P H Y R
J I O Y X U I S I E
S R M D V A R V O P
N O V T A L I R E X
H   L Y O D T E F M
```

THE CIRCLE
IS LIKE GOD

"O God, you live forever and forever! . . . You yourself never grow old. You are forever and your years never end." Pslam 102:24a, 27 TLB

"What a God He is! How perfect in every way! All his promises prove true. He is a shield for everyone who hides behind him." Psalm 18:30 TLB

Chapter 17 — "Jonah Learns About God"

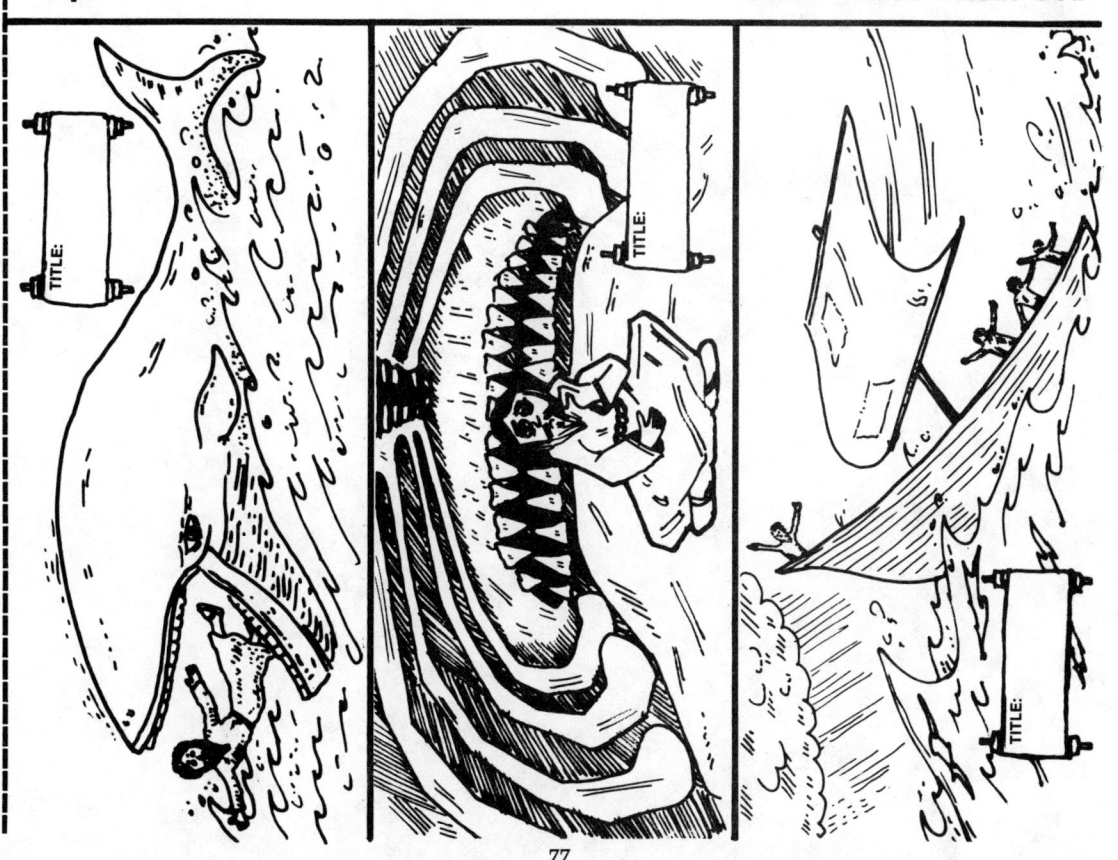

TITLE:

TITLE:

TITLE:

77

Chapter 18 — "Treasure Hunt"

TREASURE HUNT

START HERE ↓

Look up:

- Colossians 3:14
- Philippians 4:4
- John 14:27
- James 1:2-4
- Colossians 3:12
- 2 Thessalonians 1:11
- Proverbs 28:20
- Titus 3:2
- Acts 24:25

The Treasure: Galatians 5:22, 23

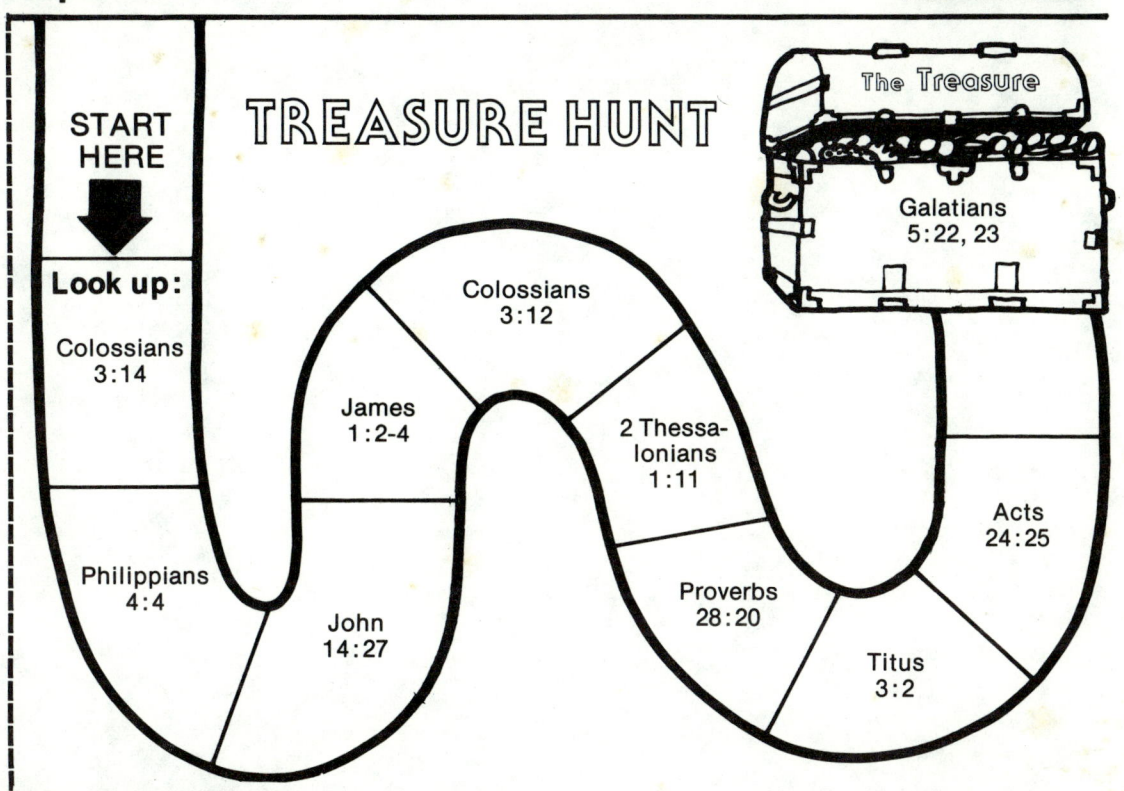

Learning Activity — "Bible Basketball"

Bible Basketball

RUNNING SCORE					
1	1	19	19	42	42
2	2	20	20	43	43
3	3	21	21	44	44
4	4	22	22	45	45
5	5	23	23	46	46
6	6	24	24	47	47
7	7	25	25	48	48
8	8	26	26	49	49
9	9	27	27	50	50
10	10	28	28		
11	11	29	29		
12	12	30	30		
13	13	31	31		
14	14	32	32		
15	15	33	33		
16	16	34	34		
17	17	35	35		
18	18	36	36		
		37	37		
		38	38		
		39	39		
		40	40		
		41	41		

TEAM	SCORE BY QUARTERS				
	1	2	3	4	F